Miracles Only Come in One Size

Lois A. Enochs

Lois A. Enochs

Insight Publishing
Sevierville, Tennessee

Miracles Only Come in One Size

10 9 8 7 6 5 4 3 2

Printed in the United States

ISBN: 1-60013-064-X

Dedication

To the summer of 1959: A time when summer days were endless, summer nights touched the soul, and full moons shined brighter. A time of drive-in movies and music that will live forever.

I bless every friend, neighbor, relative, horse, pony, dog, car, motorcycle, and mosquito of that season. I remember every sight, smell, sound, emotion, and event. I cherish the music, the laughs, and the tears of a time that can only be remembered with the heart.

Table of Contents

Chapter One

Not an Autobiography

I sit here now on that uncomfortable back side of *middle age,* experiencing one of those times we all go through now and then when we look back at life with a gasp, a sigh, and a smile for all that has transpired. Then I inevitably look toward the future with a similar gasp, sigh, and smile, and wonder if the future holds that coveted *best day of my whole life.*

There was a time when I thought people who spent a lot of time looking back or telling stories from their past were a little sad. Though I firmly believe in living in the moment, the past is where we had our joys, our sorrows, our love, and our lessons. Joy revisited is joy relived. Love remembered is love still felt. A lesson looked back on is a lesson reinforced and a sorrow brought to mind can remind us how much we have healed. The past is where we draw our pride from a *job well done* and where we harvest information to guide our present decisions.

A few years ago I began documenting some events in my life that could be referred to as lucky, coincidental, fortunate, interesting, unusual, remarkable, unbelievable, or serendipitous.

But I say that a miracle by any other name is still a miracle and miracles only come in one size. There is a charming little book called *Small Miracles;* it is a wonderful collection of stories, but I beg to differ with the terminology.

What was so "big" about parting the Red Sea? If you are homeless and hungry, the miracle may be that ten-dollar bill you find on a street down which you typically never walk. If you are a mom in a troubled relationship, it may be a dream in which your grandmother advises you on what to do that enables you to move forward with great calm and assurance.

Try thinking this way: The miracle was not the parting of the sea, the ten dollars, or the dream. The miracle is that we are provided with what we need, when we need it, in remarkable ways. In some cases our miracles prevent us from doing something that is not in our best interest, whether we realize it in the moment or not. A little bad luck for me when trying to move to Florida resulted in my moving to Europe. Need I say more? There are times when the working out of our miracle does not look like or feel like what we want and it can place us in uncomfortable situations of transition.

Though frequently confirming my faith, the experiences I share in this book caused me to question it on occasion. There were disappointments that turned into blessings, trials that exercised my soul and expanded my belief system, and miracles that baffled me. The ultimate lesson was that I walk into all situations as a co-creator with an awesome power that I am comfortable calling "God."

I am also comfortable saying I believe in miracles, angels, reincarnation, life after life, psychic abilities, and the power of our own thoughts and words to create our circumstances. It is more than a belief. I know these things because I have lived these things.

Although I have, through encouragement of friends, decided to document and share some of my experiences, this book is in no way an autobiography. I am not so sure my life even has a *story.*

Besides, I discovered my perfect autobiography already written in a copy of the *National Science of Mind Center Newsletter* in San Antonio, Texas, some time in the late 1980s. It is one of the simplest and most powerful writings I have ever encountered and I carry a tiny copy of it with me always. Seldom is so much said in so few words.

An Autobiography in Five Chapters
(National Science of Mind Center Newsletter)

C H A P T E R 1

I walk down the street.
There is a deep hole in the sidewalk.
I fall in — I am lost — I am helpless.
It isn't my fault.
It takes forever to find a way out.

C H A P T E R 2

I walk down the same street.
There is a deep hole in the sidewalk.
I pretend I don't see it.
I fall in again.
I can't believe I am in the same place.
But it isn't my fault.
It still takes a long time to get out.

C H A P T E R 3

I walk down the same street.
There is a deep hole in the sidewalk.
I see it is there.
I fall in — it's a habit — but, my eyes are open.
I know where I am.
It is my fault.
I get out immediately.

CHAPTER 4

I walk down the same street.
There is a deep hole in the sidewalk.
I walk around it.

CHAPTER 5

I walk down a different street.

— author unknown

The first thirty-five years of my life seemed to be completely driven by circumstances beyond my control. Within that time there was great joy, great heartache, intense bewilderment, a lot of hard work, and sickness. I often wondered why I experienced so many difficulties. At the same time I was keenly aware of many incredible and unusual experiences with which I had been blessed.

I needed answers. Everything just seemed to happen to me — good or bad. Why was it so difficult to create the life I wanted? The following chapters will help you understand why my faith is so strong and how certain universal principles are working in our lives whether we are aware of them or not. Understanding and believing this, simply put, gives a person control. You would not operate a heavy piece of equipment without knowing some of the rules of operation, would you?

When life corralled me into learning about karma, reincarnation, and the power of our own spoken words, flashbacks of my own life offered me unquestionable proof of it all. That just goes to show how smart God is. He knew I would be hard to convince so I had to live out all the evidence first. It is amazing how much pain can flow out when understanding flows in.

I once saw a sign on an office wall that read, *No man is my friend; no man is my enemy; every man is my teacher.* The clarity and truth in this succinct statement is powerful. From a very early age I practiced the wisdom of learning from other people's mistakes, successes, joys, and sorrows. However, it did not prevent me from encountering my own trials and tribulations. I believe it did accelerate my learning process, which advanced me to some extraordinary experiences for deeper lessons. What I did not understand during most of this process was how and why it all worked this way.

There is a wonderful expression in the metaphysical community that says, *"When the student is ready, the teacher will come."* Many teachers have come my way. I must say that many of them were well disguised — perhaps as a thoughtless relative, a seemingly psychotic supervisor, a selfish friend or deceitful co-workers. It is to my blessing that some of these lessons came through what seemed to be difficult circumstances. Many became demonstrations — miracles if you will — that everything can serve a purpose. These lessons were also confirmations that we are all guided and that every thought we have, every choice we make, and how we respond to every experience (lesson) is vital to our life path.

The majority of people on earth have some form of faith in a higher power. It takes on many names and is honored by a wide variety of ritual activities, but this unseen force is one of the most common threads running through the human race.

The conundrum of who might be right and which "God-dictated" rituals are correct was a serious and constant wonderment for me. Since I now know that what we *think on* creates our experiences, I can retrospectively see that most of the experiences in my life were designed to solve that very conundrum. My answers — my proof — came from my own life. Life had been like a puzzle that formed no clear picture until the final missing piece was in place — then my whole existence came into focus. Once the *light bulbs* starting coming on, information, special people, and circumstances flowed in and out of my life with perfect timing and great speed. Of course there were still times when the element of perfect timing went unrecognized until farther down the road. But I had enough evidence to trust and to have faith that it was indeed perfect and would work toward my higher good. And so it was.

In this book I will share with you bits and pieces of my personal evolution. What a joy it was to figure out that God is bigger and better (and nicer) than I ever thought. And what fun it was to discover that various esoteric sciences such as astrology, numerology, dreams, and psychic powers are divine resources.

I do not attempt to convince anyone of a higher power. I believe it is safe to presume that anyone reading this book already has such a belief or is looking for a reason to believe. What I do attempt is to show the incredible power that faith offers. Most importantly, I trust you will understand the power of your own mind, your thoughts, and your words. For if you *do not* understand this, it does not diminish that power but you might just misuse it or waste it like waving a pistol around not knowing it is loaded.

There are many books documenting experiences of extraordinary coincidences, demonstrations of faith, and events that any sane person might call miraculous. They are wonderful. I have read them and I have no doubt about their accuracy. However, a book of thirty or forty stories that happened to thirty or forty different people can subconsciously plant the belief that such wonderful events are extremely rare and that we might be limited to only one or two in a lifetime. Not so. The experiences in this book are all mine. If I can co-create miraculous events in my life, so can you!

I am just an ordinary, hard-working, honest person managing her way through this three-dimensional physical existence like everyone else. Many people, through their insights or their participation in my experiences, have helped me learn and grow. It is with great joy I now share some of it with you — perhaps it is your turn to learn and grow.

Chapter Two

Early Childhood

The need for some form of spiritual practice in my life has been with me as long as I can remember. Even as a small child I would hide in a closet or wiggle in between some bushes in the backyard and talk to someone or something up there in the sky about things I did not understand. There seems to be an inherent instinct within us that knows our answers come from some source *out there*. All those questions — all that need for understanding — created for me a life filled with a myriad of experiences that ultimately led me to answers.

I felt very much *at one* with a higher power. It seemed to tell me things — not that I heard voices, I just knew things that others did not.

As a child, I lived in a sixth sense world. I became very thoughtful about a lot of things. In this process I learned that I could make things happen by thinking about them or change what happened by changing what I expected. When I was around five or six a street was cut through the large yard between our house and the neighbor's house. This was a slow process and for many seasons it left a stone-filled street with smudge pots marking the soft edges of the unfinished street. The good part about this was that it left a lot of mud to play in on rainy days. The bad part was that the stones were painfully sharp to play on. This was a serious problem for me because I was always barefoot.

This little street presented me with two interesting lessons in the power of the mind. Let's face it, kids find fire very interesting and those smudge pots provided endless fascination for me. It started by just watching the flame and the black smoke sort of dancing around it. I would get close enough to smell the unusual fumes but was careful enough not to get dirty. Sooty hands would have been a dead give-away to Mom that I had been a bit too close to the flame. For some reason I liked the round shape of the smudge pots and that they were very dirty from soot. They seemed so functional and appropriate for their task. They just sat there and did their job all day and all night. They were quite personified to me.

I was particularly fond of one smudge pot on the far side of the street. I spent a lot of time sitting near it and I quickly advanced to wondering how close I could put my hand to the flame. I kept "thinking" I could get closer without it being too hot. Soon I was "thinking" I could run my hand through the flame very fast and not get too hot. Soon I was slowing down my movement through the flame and saying to myself, "It will not burn." By the time I could briefly pause my hand in the flame without it burning me, I had satisfied my interest in the smudge pot and its flame and, as children do, I moved on to other things. Forty years later, however, that same hand and fire would take me to the ultimate level in the power of the mind and faith. That story is told later.

Simultaneously with my fire fascination a similar experiment was taking place. In visiting my favorite friendly smudge pot I made frequent crossings over all those stones with their pointy little edges in my bare feet. So, as I was learning to "think" the fire would not burn me, I decided to try it on the stones. I stood at the edge of the street and said, "The stones will not hurt my feet. I just won't think about it." It was no sooner said than done—I could actually run on the stones and feel almost nothing—certainly no pain. I don't know how to describe what I did with my thoughts except that I put them above my feet. Of course back then I did not look at it that way. I was just entertaining myself with how my mind and body associated. Thank God we did not have all the toys and computer games of today to effortlessly fill my mind with someone else's creativity.

What probably started me wondering if maybe my thought processes or perceptions might be a little different from others' was when I got in trouble in the third grade for telling all my classmates that our teacher was going to have a baby. Actually it was Mrs. Johnson (not her real name) who got in trouble because the word got to the principal before she had time to tell him. Eventually Mrs. Johnson had a few things to say to me about the situation. She herself had just found out and she wanted to know how I knew. I had no answer for her because I just knew. It seemed obvious to me but I could not express why. It was no different than noticing if someone was happy or sad. So, as a third grader I began keeping things I "knew" to myself. It then became a great curiosity to me to try to figure out when people knew the same things I did and when they did not. If I could not formulate a good explanation for my conclusions, I kept them to myself until I figured out if they were things others knew or not. This began a life of keeping pretty much everything to myself. I became an observer of everything and everyone and found it quite interesting.

Certainly I did not become an introvert. I remained very active and I had a good sense of humor; but only a small amount of who I was, what I thought, and what I wanted was ever exposed. This was very comfortable for me. These things belonged inside.

It was not until 1986 that my life underwent a complete spiritual transformation. Not until then would I speak of certain events in my life and begin to study the laws of cause and effect that rule us. Only then did I start to make sense out of my life and the lives of those around me. Hundreds of past experiences became overwhelming evidence that my new knowledge was *truth*.

Ultimately, it is just a choice we make as to whether or not we go down new paths. But *one* foot on that path of greater understanding is all it takes. You will never leave it. You may walk slowly or set an Olympic pace—your choice. Albert Einstein once said, "A mind expanded to a greater idea can never return to its original size." Once you step on the spiritual path, there is no going back. More questions will haunt you and more answers will come. Suddenly all the people you meet will be interested in the same subject matter, but they will know more than you do and will assist you in amazing ways.

Let's talk about the "path" for a minute. Even though I had limitless faith in a higher power and a life after this one, I certainly was not on any path until about 1984 at the age of thirty-seven. I would not realize I was on a "path" until 1986. During those two years I seemed to have no control over my life. I know now that the Universe took over and gave me very few options until I went in the right direction. I was herded as surely as a sheepdog herds a wandering sheep until I was right where I belonged. I also know now that I could have avoided several of the more difficult years of my life had I been more open to information and people coming into my life. But like most people I just kept trying to *make* myself and everyone else happy according to my old blueprint of what I wanted happiness to be. However, I kept asking for help so the Universe kept doing whatever was necessary to get me to try a new approach. It was time to *walk down a different street*.

It is so important to understand the incredible power we have over our own lives. There will always be difficult issues to deal with—stuff happens—but we should be able to get through a sad or difficult time without being an unhappy person. The kind of entanglements, worry, and guilt that make us unhappy are not necessary.

There are many disciplines of study to help guide us. I believe the magic element in finding personal peace is to find understanding. Before understanding must come knowledge. The more doors of knowledge you open, the more channels the Universe has through which to work its wonders for you. The more awareness you have of metaphysical energies and activity, the more you see how synchronized the Universe is. That will strengthen your faith and your strengthened faith will bring you better results. In my years of metaphysical studies and providing spiritual advice I have encountered so many people who look for the *one* answer or the *one* area of study that is *the* answer or *the* path assuring them a better life. I propose that you need to know many things about many disciplines. I also propose that this does not have to be overwhelming. It does not have to be done today or even tomorrow. It is a life-long process. If you have a true desire to "tune in" and let the Universe help you make good decisions and smooth out the bumps in your road, there are many things you need to know and understand. Seek and ye shall find.

It is easy to be looking so hard for an answer through one door that you do not notice the perfect solution tapping on a window trying to get in. There are infinite sources for answers. A talent that is wise to develop is that of receiving information through all doors, windows, and under the carpet. I once read a bumper sticker that said, "I found Jesus. He was behind the sofa the whole time." Also, be open to receiving guidance through your eyes, your ears, your heart, and your gut.

Many of you are most likely familiar with the story about the man who was caught in a flood:

> As the water started getting dangerously high, rescue vehicles drove the streets with sirens warning everyone to pack only a few essentials and leave their homes for higher ground. The gentleman stayed in his home quite confident that God would save him. Some time later, after the water had caused the man to retreat to his second floor, a neighbor came by in his boat saying,

*"Please share our boat. The water is getting much higher." The man once again responded with appreciation, but declined the ride stating that God would save him. It wasn't long until he was climbing out of his second story window to the roof. As he sat, praying to be saved, a helicopter flew over dropping a rescue rope for him. He waved them away calling out that his faith was still strong and he believed God would save him. With the water at his feet and no higher to climb, he asked, "God, why have you forsaken me? I have demonstrated incredible faith yet you have not responded." With that, God replied, "What do you mean I have not responded? I sent sirens, a boat, and a helicopter. **What were you waiting for?"***

For starters, it is important to understand that there is one power and one power only and that every molecule is filled with that energy. Not just you, but your clothes, your desk, your plants, your kitchen counters, your thoughts, and your words. Our understanding of that energy and our use of it determine the results in our life. Faith in that power works like an afterburner on a jet engine—kicking in extra power when you need it. What you think is what you get. If your faith is in Murphy's Law, guess what you get. If your core belief is that all things work toward good, guess what you get.

The Universe and everything in it is made up of energy. The energy fields of your desk, your clothes, and the orbiting planets all have an influence. Most importantly, your personal creative power comes from your thoughts, your words, and your faith. Get a true grasp of how this works and combine it with a thorough understanding of reincarnation and you will have "the bull by the horns."

First, make a decision to take control of your life and put the first foot on that metaphysical path. As I have said often and to many, "Put your boat in the water and God will steer it." You will be in the right place at the right time as the path unfolds beneath your feet. Perhaps you will be trying to decide if you should start by studying astrology or visualization, then tomorrow morning the person on the bus beside you is reading *The Only Way to Learn Astrology, Volume I.* You get the idea. That is where the faith part is so critical. **Know** that your answers will come—do not hope, wish, or think maybe. Trust that you will be led in the right direction and if you need to change direction, something will come along and cause you to make that change. You must be ready to accept the changes that come. They may be very different from what you had been planning and if you have been too far off track they can temporarily appear more like a setback than a blessing. Know what you want but do not be so specific that you restrict yourself from a higher good. Do not limit the Universe. This reminds me of another old story:

> *There was a man of great faith who had his heart set on a new Volkswagen. He prayed with great diligence and faith, pleading that he would never ask for another thing if he could just get his Volkswagen. He prayed for opportunities to make enough money to buy a Volkswagen. He would pass a Volkswagen on the road and visualize himself in it. He reminded God that this was a modest car and a reasonable request. Finally the day came when the man got his Volkswagen. With great appreciation he turned to God and said, "Thank you for my Volkswagen." God replied, "Not a problem, but what I had in mind for you was a new Cadillac."*

Many good people have lost faith because of a lack of understanding of how prayer works and how the immense power of our own consciousness and intentions create circumstances in our life. I would love to clear up some of that for you.

Throughout this book you will find repeated within my experiences that the right people, the right circumstances, and the right books will come our way at the right time. But it must be your intention to find answers and you must be open to receiving them. They will come in the most unexpected ways and they might not be the answer you want. But I assure you they will be the best answers. A spiritual path is not unlike driving down a highway. There are road signs you must read for a safe journey and detour signs to keep you from going into dead ends. There are other drivers on your road and approaching your road. To some we yield and for others we stop. Some must be passed or you will never get where you want to go. There are interesting sights along the road that enrich the journey but only if you observe them. Open your eyes, read the signs, and drive safely!

Chapter Three

A Glimpse of the Other Side

The following event remains as clear in my mind as if it happened yesterday, complete with sounds and colors. Never again would I feel ordinary or small. Never again would I be without purpose or feel alone. This event became my strength— my *secret* power of survival.

I was hospitalized for surgery in the fall of 1968 when I was twenty-one years old. Though the procedure went well, a lack of proper post-operative care from the night nurse caused me serious agony throughout my first night in the hospital. Before two weeks would pass, my heart and soul would be changed forever.

With one look at me on the morning after surgery my doctor knew there was a problem. I was crying so hard while telling him about my night that he could hardly understand me. As soon as he got the idea of what had happened he excused himself and left the room. He came back with one of those heavenly shots that makes all the pain go away and puts you right to sleep. I later learned that while he was getting the shot he also took time to make sure I never saw that nurse again (nor did anyone else) and the other nurses were instructed to keep a close eye on me for infection.

After that rocky start my recovery took a turn toward normal. Aside from an expected amount of pain I thought I was doing well. In fact, I felt well enough to help an elderly lady who shared my room for a couple of days. I do not remember what her condition was but I certainly remember her poor eyesight. Every time I got out of bed (in my white hospital gown), or even sat up, she would ask me to raise her bed, lower her bed, get her some water, or whatever need was on the end of her tongue just waiting for a nurse. I also remember her impaired hearing. When I tried to explain I was a patient and not a nurse she could not hear me and just repeated her list of needs. She obviously thought I was a nurse. She was such a sweet soul that it was easier to help her out for a few days until she went home. Besides, I thought the moving around would be good for me.

After several days in the hospital I was missing my two-and-a-half-year-old daughter terribly. Fortunately, I was on the ground floor of the hospital with a window right beside my bed. I had my family bring her to the window so I could see her and we could wave and blow kisses. It was just what I needed to get me through the last day or two that I expected to be in the hospital.

Soon the morning of my release was at hand. That morning I did not mind waking up early to the routine and commotion of the hospital staff. I wanted to be ready to go home as soon as the doctor made his visit and signed the release. My day nurse was very good. As she was greeting me good morning, setting out my pills, and freshening my water I was doing my best to wake up from a medicated sleep. While having a nice morning chat with the head nurse about being released there was a sudden and sharp pain in my back. The surprise of it caused me to grab my back and let out a loud groan.

The concern from the nurse was immediate—she wanted to know where I hurt and how long I had been hurting. I told her it was probably just from sleeping in a poor position. But she was out of the room in a flash and very quickly someone arrived to take me to X-ray and the blood lab. I thought it was a little unnecessary but I went along. Before they could even get me back to my room I was so sick I needed help getting into the bed. I had no idea what was wrong. I was already in so much pain and chilled with fever that all I could do was get back into bed, pull the covers over me, and sleep.

The next five days and nights blended into one. Between the fever and drugs I was continually in and out of sleep and did not even know if it was day or night. Although I could not respond to anyone or communicate anything that made sense, everything was very clear inside my head. I heard and understood everything. When I tried to speak I would think all the right words, but then babbled nonsensically. There were times when I actually laughed at what I heard coming out of my mouth. Then I would try again and laugh even harder. Imagine how completely delirious I must have *appeared* to others. Babble—laugh. Babble—laugh harder. Then it was right back to sleep.

Since my thoughts were clear I was aware of the fact that I had an extremely high fever. Not only was I aware of how I felt, I could also hear people talking about my dangerously high temperatures. I had a great sense of urgency to somehow take some charge of my own care. My own personal healing method for fever had always been to *sweat it out*. When you sweat, the fever breaks. I needed blankets—lots of blankets. But how to communicate this was no small task.

I repeatedly went through exaggerated shivering motions as I bundled myself in my sheet and one of the ladies finally figured out I was cold. I was pretty pleased with my accomplishment. However, another nurse told her all the blankets were still in storage for the summer. So I had to continue my antics long enough for them to believe this was worth going to the storeroom. It was October and time to do so anyway.

Eventually I was given a *few* blankets under which I stayed until my chills turned to warmth and my warmth turned to sweat. My fever would come down and I would sleep what seemed like a brief while, then I would wake up with another high fever. The process repeated itself for days.

While hiding under my blankets I did everything I could to keep my mind alert and awake for the longest periods of time possible. It was truly scary to hear and understand what was going on around me, to know my brain was obviously in danger, and not be able to communicate anything to anyone. I intuitively knew I had to keep my mind very busy or I might lose my thinking ability. I lay there for hours on end mentally reciting everything I had ever memorized in my whole life. I sang dozens of songs, recited poems, and countless Bible verses. When I would feel myself fading into dizziness or sleep I would recite faster or try to sing out loud. That must have sounded marvelous to anyone listening. I felt as if I were fighting for my life and if I let my mind go to sleep it may never wake. Obviously there were times when I slept. I seldom knew day from night and had no idea how much time had passed. I seemed to only be getting worse each day. I could tell from conversations around me that they were only trying to keep me comfortable and calm. I would later learn they did not expect me to pull out of this.

On the fifth day something changed. I was lying there perfectly still with my arms to my sides and was thinking that I really did not feel so sick anymore. I was actually very comfortable. By the time these thoughts had totally registered I noticed that everything looked very black. My eyes were closed so I expected everything to appear sort of black, but this was about a thousand times blacker than any black I had ever seen. It was pure, solid, quite beautiful actually, and impossible to describe. In the peace and comfort of this blackness a gentle awareness came over me. I said to myself, "Oh, I know what this is. This is death." Curiously, I was perfectly calm.

I felt very peaceful and not the least bit frightened, but I was still marveling at this incredible blackness. Then something even more astonishing happened. Two black hands appeared. My analytical mind was amazed. I was trying to figure out how I could distinguish these very, very black hands from all the other blackness. It was unbelievably "black-on-black." There was no outline of the hands. Yet I saw shape, depth, and movement. I understand now that I was seeing in a dimension I had never experienced. These hands appeared centered above my face, thumbs together and palms toward me. They moved without touching me, up over my head, then separated and came around the sides of my face and repositioned in front of me with thumbs touching. They again moved up over the top of my head, around the sides of my face and repositioned as before.

As a third pass was completed, I involuntarily rose up out of my bed and up toward the ceiling. I was quite aware of being very high in the room. I actually was ducking my head and wondering why I was not bumping my head on the ceiling. When I looked down, I could tell I was much higher than the ceiling level. As I was looking down and around the room I noticed a bed with a young lady lying in it. After looking at her for a moment I calmly realized I was the young lady and I understood that I had died and left my body. My subsequent thought was that "she" did not really look quite as I had always thought "I" looked. It occurred to me that we never really do see our own faces. The reflection in the mirror provides us only with a slightly distorted image of what we look like. I was seeing myself as others had.

As I lingered somewhere above my hospital room I began to know everything there was to know. I understood the origin of the universe. I *knew* God, understood life, and why each person existed. The knowledge of complicated mathematics and other sciences filled my head and I felt great joy from understanding all things. Numbers were the language for most of this understanding. All things were mathematically correct with endless but understandable formulas. I read lengthy formulas as rhythmically as reading a beautifully constructed sentence. In my consciousness I saw shelves and shelves of books and smiled with elation as their contents just seemed to jump into my mind. I absorbed knowledge at light speed. I knew all things and all things were in perfect synchronization. I was a part of all things and they a part of me. As exciting as this was, it also began to feel right and familiar — as if I had been there before.

I did not dwell on my physical body for any length of time. It was a very unemotional experience to look at it. It was as objective as taking off a coat, laying it down, then turning around and looking at it. However, as I looked about the room, the window on the far wall caught my attention. This quickly brought my thoughts back to the memory of my daughter visiting me at the window throwing me kisses and reaching out to have me hold her. Now I was not so objective. I had thoughts of her being left behind without me and wondered what might happen to her. I quickly thought, "God, please send me back to raise my daughter." (I followed my request with a promise that remains between me and God.) I instantly swooped downward and back into my body just as I had left. I was once again lying in the bed, very calm and still. The incredible blackness was still there — blackness that would make ebony appear to be off-white. There were no black hands. I knew I was alive and I knew why.

I lay there with my eyes closed observing the depths of this blackness. From within it came a white hand — only a right hand. This marvelous white color was as far beyond our scale of white as the black had been beyond our scale of black.

After appearing and remaining stationary for a few moments, this right hand began a similar motion as before. It moved upward and over the top of my head, then moved to its right, came around the left side of my face, and returned to its original position. It did not touch me. It made a second pass over my face above my head and around the side of my face and returned. It did not touch me. It made a third pass over my face and up over my head. The hand gently touched me with the tip of its center finger as it moved down the side of my face. The touch began at my temple and came to rest at the center of my chin where it paused for a moment before returning to its position above my face.

I knew without doubt that I had just been touched by the hand of Christ. I knew I was healed and that it was perfectly safe to just fall asleep and rest. I took a deep breath and slept.

I woke up from my nap feeling better physically than I had ever felt at any given moment in my life. I have no idea if I had slept for ten minutes or ten hours but I woke up completely well. Not only did I not have a fever but I was clear of mind and speech. I had complete strength—there was no weakness. I had undergone major surgery, battled a serious kidney infection, and woke up as if I were in perfect health and had never been sick a day in my life.

I told the nurse to get my doctor on the phone because I was ready to go home. Needless to say, they were quite amazed and just wanted me to lie down and rest. I finally convinced them to call the doctor and he promised to see me as soon as he got to the hospital. He was quite perplexed and let me know that he was actually amazed to see me conscious, but he felt sure I was not strong enough to go home. I did not tell him about my experience, however I did say, "You don't understand. I'm healed. I really am ready to go home." We struck a deal. If I felt just as well the next morning I could go home. Of course I went home the following day!

Even now, a few decades later, it is impossible to look at my daughter without knowing that my love for her is what saved my life. She became my purpose—the reason I was sent back.

I have come to believe that we choose the time of our departure no matter how untimely it may seem to others. There are various points within each life where we have opportunities to leave. At a time of emotional and physical difficulty my subconscious had accepted one of those opportunities but subsequently chose to return when reminded of my daughter. Certainly there comes a time when our specific karma *requires* us to make our final transition. My personal theory is that any time we transition before our karmic mission for this life is complete we are able to pause and reconsider. Believe me, there is nothing quite like being in another dimension to give you pause, and nothing like a beautiful baby girl to make you reconsider.

Chapter Four

Footprints in the Snow

It was late December 1969 and our modest Christmas tree was standing in front of the living room window. Snow was falling and I was glad to be home and inside for the snowy weekend ahead. I loved my weekends. For two full days I did not have to leave my bright, curly-headed little girl for work.

Although the holiday expressed itself all around me, the Christmas spirit would soon escape me as if oozing right through the pores of my skin. The past five years had been so physically and financially difficult that in one moment, all of the effort, exhaustion, heartache, and sadness came crashing in as though it had all happened at once.

Let me back up a little and set the proper scene for how I went from a very difficult situation to one of the most, if not *the* most, wonderful experiences of my life. I share this situation not to evoke sympathy in any fashion. My difficult times are the very foundation of who I am as well as what enabled me to have some of my most incredible demonstrations of faith.

I was a single parent and my daughter was now almost four years old. It was the 1960s so the social and psychological issues of single parenting were difficult enough, but the finances were a very critical issue. In order to have a secure job, I worked at a military installation and drove one hundred and four miles round trip each day. The winters in Ohio were much more severe back then, and at times I would leave as early as five o'clock in winter months to get to the babysitter, pick up all my carpoolers, and get us all to work by eight o'clock.

My fixed annual expenses (rent, electric, phone, etc.) were two dollars less than my annual net income. This did not include groceries or clothes for my daughter, and certainly no extras. From the money I made on my carpool, I bought gas and had a budget of five dollars per week for groceries. There were times I had to take a sick day from work to save the two dollars gas and two and a half dollars sitter expenditures for the day in order to meet expenses.

Lunch during the workday was certainly out of the question. An evening meal might consist of a nineteen-cent TV dinner for my daughter, and I would have the last bite or two she did not finish. I remember feeling painfully guilty for the times I hoped she would not be very hungry—leaving more for me. Other times, groceries for the workweek might be one pack of ten breakfast sausage links and five small potatoes. For dinner we each had one sausage link and half of a baked potato.

Conditions were not financially tight just here and there. This was how we lived in those early years. The slightest unexpected expense was devastating. My daughter seldom had the benefit of seeing a doctor when she was ill and I developed a severe case of anemia which later required two years of vitamin and mineral injections to bring me back to health.

I actually had a semi-necessary surgical procedure just because I carefully calculated that after payment from both of my insurance policies I would have an extra sixty dollars. I needed two new tires and this was my best plan to come up with the money. This was my life. I had responsibilities and I met them.

With the scene set, I come back to the real story:

Christmas was close and I looked forward to the weekend. It was payday Friday and I went through the ritual I had repeated every two weeks for years: I picked up my daughter, came home and got my check from the mailbox, went to the bank, and asked the friendly young teller for all small bills. I went immediately home to manage my budget. In the middle of my living room floor I made six little piles of money. On one pile I would place a two-week portion of my annual rent, on another a two-week share of my annual car payment, on another a two-week share of my annual average electric bill, and so on through my expenses. This particular Friday, my bills were already there to be paid, so I knew exactly what was due.

I got down on my knees and leaned over my clearly designated piles and began the familiar process of sorting my wages. As I came to the end, I had a little problem. The last pile (my water bill as I recall) was for about eight dollars and there I sat with my last five dollars in my hand. Here, after four long years, I was three dollars short. Forget that there was nothing to live on for the next two weeks. I was used to that. But for the first time I had a bill that could not be paid. I was heartsick. I feared the water company might turn off my water or that someone might try to take my daughter away if I could not pay the bills. It was truly a different time back then. I was twenty-three years old and lived in a very small world between being at work and at home with my daughter. For years I had been doing the impossible, and doing it with a smile to the outside world. Only in those precious personal moments between when my daughter was tucked in bed and when I went to sleep, did I allow myself the tears it took to let a little of the pressure and pain escape. But now, after years of *managing*, the mental and emotional fortitude that had sustained me just vanished. Fear and fatigue won out on this snowy December night and I cried out, "Dear God, help me." I burst into tears and could not see or think beyond this discouraging moment.

My daughter heard me crying and came running. She dropped to her knees and went into action as if she were an EMS worker at the scene of an accident. "Here, Mommy. Let me wipe your tears." With bright eyes and all the confidence in the world, she held my face in her hands and wiped my tears with her little thumbs. "Now everything is fine," she proclaimed. This was something I had always done for her when she cried. I always told her it was magic and it made tears disappear. Not only did it work, I had to do it *every* time she cried. Talk about the power of suggestion!

Suddenly, I felt very lucky. I have never felt more loved than during those few moments with those little thumbs working diligently under my eyes, absolutely *knowing* it would make the tears go away. I put my arms around her, took a deep breath, and hugged her tightly. The tears began to subside. It *was* magic.

Early that evening a storybook-type snowfall had begun and by now the snow was about a foot deep. So in the moment I decided to take delight in the beauty of our simple Christmas tree standing in the corner, the gentle snowfall, and the wonderful little cherub I was holding in my arms.

After those few moments of simultaneous joy and sorrow, there was a knock on the door. I lifted my daughter to her feet and got myself up off the floor. I was a little surprised since I seldom had company and the weather was so bad. Trying to look presentable, I patted my face, found a smile, and opened the door—there stood a gentleman, the likes of which I had never seen. He wore layers of tattered clothing, his hair and skin looked weathered, and his eyes were an unforgettable blue. There was a cardboard sign hanging around his neck on a string of twine that identified him as being diabetic, almost blind, and a deaf-mute. His eyes never left mine. Half of my mental awareness was consumed just taking in the visual impression of this being. Hollywood would have been proud to create this particular character. I have often wished I could paint just to recreate his image. Yet somehow he did not seem unclean or unhealthy. He overwhelmed my senses.

He handed me a plastic container of sewing needles that I assumed he was selling and a card about the size of a business card. The card pictured the sign language alphabet. As my hands met his, I noticed I still had that last five-dollar bill in my right hand. A sense of calm came over me, and as naturally as breathing I placed this last bill in his hands. I gestured that he should also keep the needles. He ever so slightly shook his head no, placed the needles and the card in my hands, and moved my hands back toward me. All the while, his nearly translucent blue eyes remained fixed on mine. I smiled, said something very unoriginal like "Bless you," and reluctantly closed the door.

As the door closed I felt thankful for being in a small but *warm* home. I recalled an old Bible quote and thought to myself, *"Oh well, it will return ten fold."* Instantly the idea came to me to have this unfortunate, yet captivating man inside for a cup of hot chocolate and to warm up. I turned quickly to reopen the door, but he was not there. It had been less than five seconds since I had bid him farewell with "Bless you," and he was *not* there.

He was nowhere in sight, yet I kept looking up and down the street as if my eyes were deceiving me. My porch light was on and the entire area glowed as the streetlights reflected off the new, deep, undisturbed snow. I stood in my doorway unable to stop looking. All I saw were the lighted windows of homes up and down the street where people were settled in for an evening of snow.

I closed the door, but before getting two or three steps away I returned to look up and down the street once more. Standing in the doorway I had thoughts like: How could he have gotten to a neighbor's house and been invited inside that quickly? *He couldn't.* How could he have gotten far enough away for me not to see him? *He couldn't.* Although terribly puzzled, I took a moment to delight in the beauty of the bright snow under the streetlight on the corner. That is when I saw something that brought my already puzzled thought processes to a complete standstill. *Footprints.* In all the beautiful, undisturbed new snow, there were deep, fresh footprints. Footprints which very clearly *started* just past my neighbor's house *right in the middle of the block* and came directly to my door, at my feet, where I was standing. There was no evidence of anyone turning and walking away.

I closed the door and stood there mystified and awestruck. I opened the door for another quick look. The perfectly undisturbed footprints were still there. They still started in the middle of nowhere and they still ended at my door. His Manual Alphabet card and needles were still in my hand.

The rest of the evening was spent with this gentleman on my mind. I especially thought of his eyes. I kept replaying every detail over and over in my thoughts. How tattered he looked, how rough and leathered his hands were, yet how gently he touched me and how calm he made me feel. I knew something very special had happened to me, that it was good, and that it brought me comfort. I also knew I could not speak of it to anyone.

Saturday

The next day my daughter and I went through the motions of our usual Saturday. She played while I did housework and watched some television. But at the start of the day, I couldn't resist the temptation to look outside. The footprints were still there but softened with new snow. Still starting in the middle of the block and still ending at my front door.

I was dusting my small telephone stand when the phone rang. I answered the phone as I sat down on the end of the sofa. It surprised me to hear an unfamiliar man's voice on the other end.

This unfamiliar voice identified himself as being with my insurance agency and asked me if I had received my dividend check this year. I wasn't even sure what he meant. I was also a little confused that this person was calling me. My family had used the same insurance agent ever since I could remember. He came personally to our homes to collect the payments and always took time to visit a bit. I didn't even know there were other agents at the company. I asked the caller why my agent wasn't calling about this. Our agent was getting up in years and I was concerned that something might have happened.

In lieu of an answer he said, "Well, did you get your dividend *last* year?" I assured him I had never received a dividend from the agency and he eagerly said he would check into it and get back with me. I was almost afraid to consider that this meant they owed me money.

Sunday

The plan for the day was to play and build a snowman in the back yard. Not too far into the day, I heard a car in front of the house. I looked out the front door window and saw a man I did not know coming toward my door. My assumption was that he had the wrong house so I opened the door and greeted him before he even got to my porch. I was about to ask whom he was looking for, when he inquired, "Miss Enochs?"

He was the gentleman from the insurance company who had called me only yesterday. He said he was so concerned that I had not received my dividend checks that he had a check prepared right away to cover both years and decided to deliver it to me personally. I expressed my obvious appreciation, wished him a good day, and closed the door. I looked at the check and it was for fifty-eight dollars and some change!

It had been less than two days since I had cried, "Dear God, help me." I was tired and so willing to cast my burden. I had needed eight dollars for the water bill and the five dollars for the stranger at the door had indeed returned ten fold, for a curiously precise total of fifty-eight dollars.

Feeling both bewildered and blessed, I knew this to be an experience I should just tuck away in my memory and in my heart to take out and cherish when I needed it. It was far too private and unbelievable to share. However, my curiosity would not totally leave it alone. The following week I picked up the business card of the man who had delivered the check. Having no idea what I would say, I called the insurance company and asked to speak with him. They informed me that they had no one by that name. I said, "Thank you," I hung up, and placed his card by the phone. I had to wonder if this series of events could possibly get any more confusing.

Later that day I was looking at the sign language card given to me by my blue-eyed stranger. There were moments when I needed to see it as proof this really happened. I decided to keep it with the business card of the insurance agent. I walked over by the phone where I had left his card and it was not there. It was never found and I was never able to remember his name.

Eighteen years passed before I shared this experience with anyone. By then my daughter was grown and I was living in San Antonio, Texas. I was in a metaphysical study group and one evening I arrived early and was having a nice talk with Joyce, the leader of our group. Out of nowhere I felt a desire to share this story with her before anyone else arrived. When I got to the part about the footprints she just smiled and said, "He was an angel." Joyce would become my greatest spiritual mentor and one of the jewels in my life.

It was a great moment for me to finally share this story. It was like living it all over again. The validation of having someone hear and understand this event was powerful for me. She calmly looked at me and smiled as she again said, "He was an angel."

There have been very few days in my life when I have not thought about this experience. Seldom does anyone knock on my door and enter my home without a mental image of this special visitor preceding them.

Chapter Five
The Night People

I am including this chapter about what I refer to as my *Night People* because I believe there may be some readers with similar experiences. Occasionally, when we open up to receive energy and guidance from another dimension, some difficult energies come through. Although this does not exactly fit into my theme of miracles, it seemed miraculous to me at the time to be able to control the situation. If there is only one other person reading this who is having a similar experience, this becomes a very important chapter.

Between the years of 1984 and 1994, I was repeatedly visited by strange, dark energy beings. Imagine entities of oblong shape about three or four feet long with the color and density of a very dark rain cloud. They move about effortlessly and with great energy. They communicate in a way that you cannot quite see or hear, but you are very aware of what they are thinking or saying. Mostly they laugh a taunting laugh. Even as I approach putting this experience on paper, my stomach is in a knot and I do not look forward to recalling these details.

My *Night People* episodes would happen soon after I fell asleep or even as I was drifting off. Anywhere from three to five of these beings would come to me. The first thing I would always do is count them. I suppose it is a natural defense mechanism to know what you are up against. In my dream-like, falling-asleep state, these entities would enter my bedroom at great speed and then dash about up in the ceiling area. Two or three would pull me out of bed and proceed to toss me about the room. Sometimes they would toss me to each other, but mostly they would hurl me up against the wall or the ceiling. As I bounced off the wall, another would catch me and toss me in another direction.

This would go on for what seemed like hours. I was frightened, hurting, and forever struggling to get away. They did not seem to touch me—it was more of an overpowering magnetic pull toward them as I was yanked from my bed. They were ameba-like in shape, without arms or hands, but they did seem to have a top, a bottom, a front, and back that was defined primarily by gesture and movement. I would pull as hard as I could to get away but it was a strange mental and emotional "pulling" away. Any physical effort to fight, pull away, or protect myself was futile—I could not physically move. I could feel their energies pulling and pushing me, and that energy seemed to make my body immobile, almost like being wrapped tightly in a blanket. The entire time I would be thinking that I had to *wake up* to get away. As they flung me around I frantically tried to move and scream. I had to do whatever it took to become totally awake. I had to get myself away from their *pull* to come back to a conscious state. Over the years I learned that waking up was the only way out, but in the process I learned some other things.

Sometimes when I broke free and fell from the ceiling area back to my bed, I woke up just before landing in the bed. My covers were usually a mess or sometimes not even on the bed. My body hurt all over and I even had some bruises where I made contact with the walls in this nocturnal battle.

There were times when I could feel these entities approaching as I was falling asleep. I would immediately begin my fight to stay awake. As I shook off my sleepiness, I could see my hands and arms gripping the covers and my body moving slowly across the bed, dragging covers along, as they tried to pull me up. I mentally shouted, "I'm awake. I'm awake. Go away!" I was only able to communicate with them on the mental plane. This was my nightlife several nights a week and sometimes several nights in a row.

There did not seem to be much I could do about this. I was deep in my metaphysical studies and beliefs and was living the best possible life I could, yet this *dark* thing was happening to me. In all my studies and study groups, I had never heard of anything so negative and frightening as this ever happening to anyone. I was just plain scared. After a "visitation" (as I called them), I would leave my bedroom and try to sleep the rest of the night sitting in a chair in the living room. Sometimes I would rest on the couch.

When morning came, I adjusted my reality. I would immediately get busy with my morning routine. I listened to music or recited my daily affirmations—anything to separate the mind from what had happened in the night. I fully understood the power of thoughts and I would simply not let my thoughts wander that way.

One beautiful summer weekend I drove from Dallas down to San Antonio to visit friends. I think the trip was essentially to get out of my apartment and sleep somewhere else. For the past week or so I had visits several times a night, but only when I was in my bed. If only I had made that discovery earlier!

A friend I often tried to visit on trips to San Antonio was an elderly psychic whom I will refer to as Millie. While with Millie I burst into tears and told her there was something I needed to talk about. She was quite surprised and frankly so was I. It just popped out of me. It was not something I had decided to do. With great concern she said, "My goodness, Lois. What is the problem?" Words and tears flew out of me at an equal rate. My heart ached, my mind was weary, and years of this incredible torment came rushing out.

By the time I had said enough to give Millie the general idea of what was happening, I noticed her concerned look had turned into a gentle smile and then she started to laugh. This was exactly what I had tried to avoid for ten years. This was the reason I never told anyone. Then she said, "Lois, why in all these years have you never told me about this? This is not a big problem to solve." Hearing this, I exhaled with relief. I was not sure if it was because I believed her or if it was just a purging of emotions from talking about it out loud for the first time.

Millie proceeded to tell me a story about a little five-year-old boy who was brought to her by a neighbor who was close to the child's mother. Apparently the young boy had always had a sleeping problem—he hated to go to sleep, he hated getting in his bed, and he would get up in the night and run to his mother. They tried to reason with him but whenever they tried to get him to go to bed he would cry and say, "No, the peoples will come, the peoples will come." The lady who brought the boy to Millie had been a client of hers for some time and was hoping that Millie could perceive the source of the problem. The "peoples" the child described sounded like very close relatives to the "peoples" in my visitations.

I was intrigued by the story and had great compassion for that little boy. Suddenly I was not alone and I did not have to wonder if I was crazy or if I deserved these extremely difficult experiences. I was in the presence of someone who at least thought she could help me and I shared this experience with a small child who certainly had done nothing to deserve this. If they could come to him, why not me, and why not others?

Millie explained that there are disembodied entities who are not so pleasant. They will enter into any world that is open to them. For several years I had been meditating daily and was doing psychic readings where spirits often came with messages for their loved ones. Simply put, I was an open door they could come through. Small children are extremely open to these energies. I did not expect to meet such difficult energies while attempting to be my best.

Millie asked, "Where do they visit you? Is it everywhere you go or just at home?"

I answered, "No. They actually only visit me in my bedroom."

"Lois, go home and get a big saltshaker and pour salt all around the perimeter of your room and across the doorway. That will keep them away."

Now I was the one who wanted to laugh—this sounded more like a parlor trick. It seemed too simple to be true. But what was true was that my mind and body were completely drained. In a matter of minutes I had released a ten-year agony and found a potential solution. Why had I not asked sooner?

I stopped in a store before making my trip back to Dallas to buy an extra large container of salt—I did not want to take any chances. I arrived home late Sunday evening and filled my largest saltshaker and went to work. It was only about an eleven-by-eleven foot room that I needed to put salt around but it seemed as though I salted for an hour. I went around the room, then around it again, and then decided a third time around could not hurt. I moved furniture, crawled under furniture, and salted the tops of furniture. I salted shelves in the closet. I put so much salt in the doorway that it looked like a string of white ant hills. Then I decided a dash of salt in the open floor areas could not hurt. There was nothing left to do but try it. It felt a little bit like a "test drive" when I got in bed. I just lay there with my eyes wide open. I felt as if I were expecting something when in actuality I was expecting *nothing*. It is a strange feeling—waiting for *nothing* to happen. Nothing would be wonderful.

I would love to say I had a great night's sleep—but no. However, I did have a great night. My nocturnal enemies never arrived, but I kept waking up all night from apprehension.

To bring the story to a wonderful end, the only thing that disturbed my sleep for the next six months was a Dallas thunderstorm from time to time. At about the six-month mark I was falling asleep one night and sensed them coming. I jumped out of bed and did my salt routine. After that incident, I faithfully, though more moderately, replenished the salt after each vacuuming, and I have not seen the little devils since.

Chapter Six

Finding Places to Live

My home has always been the most treasured material element in this life to me. It was the one place I felt normal and safe. Each time I moved it was a thrill to decide where every little possession was set, hung, installed, or plugged in. Although moving can be a chore I have been amply blessed by living in so many places because I enjoy creating a pleasing home and settling in.

Even as a child I loved my home, my place, my space. I can close my eyes and still hear sounds from every childhood home. The sounds of someone opening a door, the creak of someone stepping on a particular threshold, the distinct whisper of the wind through a sagging summer window screen, the scent of honeysuckle coming in the kitchen window, and a yard fragrant with spring lilacs.

Friends have told me I have strong nesting instincts but I think I am just territorial. I like to define my space, create its energy and atmosphere, and guard it sacredly.

Intention is one of our most creative energies. I believe intention and love can summon up great support from the

Universe. Finding the perfect home over and over has been an area of consistent support from unseen forces. I also believe our words to be definitively creative in our lives. So often I have said, "I always find a great place to live." For about twenty years all I knew was that I was very lucky in finding great places to live, and now for the past twenty I have understood why.

My First Apartment

On a late spring evening, I was out for a walk with my daughter. At the time, she was barely two years old and we had been living with my parents. This particular night I walked and prayed. My prayer format has always been more of a one-sided dialogue than your typical prayer, but I was basically telling God I needed my own place, that I had no idea how I could manage it, and that He needed to figure it out for me.

As I walked, I noticed an elderly woman out sweeping her walkway. I recognized her as a teacher from one of my grade schools. She was having a little trouble, so addressing her by name I asked if I could help. She was very pleased that I knew who she was. While we chatted, I noticed a *FOR RENT* sign in her window. She explained how a number of years ago she had converted her home into a duplex and one side was currently for rent. I looked at the apartment, loved it, and told her I would take it. I had no idea how I would work out the money part of it but it felt right, and it had popped up in my face just after I had put it in the hands of the Universe. The rest fell into place like this:

The rent was sixty dollars a month. I quickly calculated that the pay increase I would receive very soon should amount to almost exactly sixty dollars a month. (Keep in mind it was almost forty years ago and sixty dollars got you a lovely apartment in one of the old, very large Midwest homes.)

I spent the next day wondering how to get a few furnishings. Within a couple of days I received a totally unexpected letter from a concerned friend giving me a gift of two hundred dollars cash. I was able to get all that I needed for two hundred and ten dollars.

After moving in and getting things set up, it did not take long to realize I needed some money to stock the kitchen with some general supplies. I had purchased pots and pans right after high school and Mother gave me a few dishes, but I needed some basics. I sat at the kitchen table and pleaded, "Please, I can't fail at this." Just then I heard my parents at the front door. They were there to tell me that the man who had bought my horse a couple of years earlier had finally paid the last one hundred and fifty dollars.

Later that night I sat outside on my new front steps. It was a beautiful early June evening. I was exhausted from the last three years of my life, yet overwhelmed with the blessings of just the past two weeks. My emotional self was hanging by a thread and my physical self was depleted. Yet that special connection I felt with God — that sense of being watched over — and my belief that all things can work toward good had just been demonstrated so profoundly. I inhaled a sense of security with every breath. Every time I turned situations over to God, I received miraculous resolutions. Every time I took a leap of faith I was provided with strong footing.

Just recently I learned (almost forty years later) that my Great Aunt Liddy had lived in that house. She had in fact lain for viewing after her death in my very living room. I also find it interesting that my daughter and I almost perished from a gas leak in that living room after living there about six months. Do I have any conclusions regarding these facts? No. But I am sure the Universe does.

This story is a wonderful example of the perfection of Divine timing when people only intend good things. The gentleman who had purchased my horse was the same man we bought him from the Christmas I was twelve. The horse was now quite old (and blind in one eye) and his previous owner just wanted to be able to see him grazing in the pasture until he died. How could we have possibly nagged this man for the money? My horse was where he should be. His new/old owner was a good man and would pay when he could. Everyone's heart was in the right place in this situation and everything worked out in perfect timing. I had the money at the best possible time, my beloved horse had the attention he deserved in his last years, and his owner fulfilled his desire to watch and care for him until the end.

The First Home I Owned (one of my favorite stories)

I had finally moved nearer to my workplace and was living in a spacious apartment with a full basement. I loved it and felt lucky to find so much space that I could afford. Unfortunately though, some situations came up in the neighborhood, and fearing it might not be safe to stay, I planned to move when the lease expired.

One lovely spring afternoon while cleaning my hardwood floors, a television commercial caught my attention. It was an ad for a special sale on mobile homes and something the announcer said made me feel he was speaking directly to me. My lease was about to expire and I believed with all my heart this was what I should do. I called for directions, grabbed my five-year-old and away we went.

It was the summer of 1971 and I was twenty-four years old. I was pretty wise in many ways, but not very experienced. With nothing more than excitement and a dream, my daughter Lisa and I bravely walked hand-in-hand into the dealer's office. This was going to be *my* biggest accomplishment in *her* whole life.

A tall, slender, blue-eyed handsome man whose name was Michael sat at the desk. I told him about seeing the ad and I wanted to look at some homes. I was very comfortable with him and he was extremely sweet and easygoing with my daughter. In fact, most of the conversations were between them. After looking at a couple of homes, Michael said, "I'll show you the one I would buy if I were staying around here." The home was brand new and had been purchased from another company that had gone out of business. It was superior in quality and fully furnished. It was the nicest one there and since it had been purchased under dire conditions, it was actually selling for less than the original dealer had paid for it.

A little piece of me wanted to be suspicious of this but I remained excited. I could see with my own eyes it was superior. I was shown all the paperwork on the home and I could actually purchase it for about two-thirds of the *cost* to the original dealer. It was gorgeous. I loved it. Lisa had already picked her room (the master bedroom which she did not get). I had some concerns about mobile home parks, but Michael told about two very new parks that were very restrictive and were quite lovely. There was not much left to say except, "I'll take it." The salesman said, "Great. I'd buy that one myself if I could. Let's sit down and fill out some paperwork."

I was so excited and felt genuinely happy. It was unfamiliar and intoxicating. Then the friendly salesman asked, "How much money would you like to put down?" A feeling of warmth flushed my body and my muscles went limp. Poor Michael was beside himself. It was immediately apparent I had not a penny to put down. I was so impressed with his concern as he fumbled for some tissue for my tears. He handed me his lunch napkins while I babbled something about being able to make payments, but not having so much as twenty-five dollars to put down. Thinking out loud I said, "There has to be a way. I know this is right."

Just then Michael, who had been leaning back on the hind legs of his chair, rocked forward, leaned across the desk, put his hand on mine and fixed his royal blue eyes on mine. He blurted out, "I know what we can do. You've got your home." In the past five minutes I had gone from a super *high* to a super *low* and I was trying to find some *middle* place where I could hear and believe what he was saying. The basic premise was that since the house was selling for less than "cost," he had room to mark the price up $2,000 and then say I made a $2,000 down payment, leaving me a balance of the price he quoted me. It sounded so simple. It worked, and I got my home.

Less than two weeks later, after my loan was approved and all arrangements had been made to deliver the home to a beautiful new mobile home park at the edge of a small town, I went back to tell the salesman how happy we were and to thank him so much for thinking of a way to make this possible. When I got there I met a different salesperson. I asked for Michael. The person on duty did not know anyone by that name. I explained that I had just met with him week before last. He said, "Oh, you must mean that drifter. He only worked here a couple of afternoons. He was just passing through and wanted to earn some money for the road. He sold one home, a shady deal that the boss wasn't happy about, and then left. He hasn't even been back to pick up his pay." I thanked the man kindly and left without another word.

So, whether there was an angel in that sales chair or a creative-thinking drifter who just happened to cross my path, it was a Divine incident. However, there were times when I could not resist comparing Michael's blue eyes to the eyes of the unforgettable stranger who knocked on my door that snowy December. By now I was starting to recognize His *mysterious ways*. And once again my sense of being watched over was strengthened.

I lived in that home in the new upscale park for four years. Then, as can happen in Ohio, there was a bad tornado season and I was ready for a house with a foundation and some brick and mortar.

The First House I Owned (with foundation, brick, and mortar)

Having never bought a house before, some of my male colleagues at work felt compelled to advise me. The general advice was, "You can't afford anything very big, so look for a small wood-frame house for about $18,000." I am pretty good with numbers and the real estate market was in the early stages of inflated interest and housing prices. This did not make much sense to me, but I never ignore the advice of people with more experience.

It did not take long to see that the older, two-bedroom, wood-frame homes at $18,000 to $20,000 were only available with new, high-interest loans and payments of about $350 a month. But what I wanted was a newer, three-bedroom, brick home with a two-car garage in a good school district.

I solicited a realtor and gave her a long list of criteria, including the type of house and desired area. I also said I wanted to assume no more than a 7 percent loan with payments of no more than $200 and I could only put $5,000 down. She said, "That's impossible. If a deal like that were out there, everyone would want it. It would only be on the market a day." My reply was simple: "Will you put it in your computer and try, or should I ask another agent?"

She was a little surprised by the resolve in my voice and being a very nice lady she agreed to try. She called me the next day at work and was so excited I could hardly understand her. We met and she showed me a list of nine homes that met my criteria. I was not nearly as surprised because it never sounded all that unreasonable to me. I was a little curious about why she was so excited. After just a few minutes together she said, "These are great deals. I'm going to sell every one of them." And she did. As for me, I got an eighteen-month-old, three-bedroom brick home on a cul-de-sac with a large lot and marble windowsills for five thousand dollars down and two hundred and two dollars per month.

The Universal principle here is that of knowing what you want, seeing it, believing it, and *knowing* it will happen. At the time I did not understand this principle and how it worked. But the laws of the Universe are at work, whether you are aware or not—whether you believe or not.

Unfortunately we can become so programmed by habit, by the way things "used to be," and by what others tell us, that we do not really stop and think through situations. If I had listened to my *experienced* colleagues' advice, or listened to my realtor, I would not have found my very first house. There is more to buying a house than the sale price. The agent was so programmed to think that good deals were very rare and were never on the market long enough to show that she never tried. She told me that I altered the whole way she ran her business. She quit trying to get listings and set out to find all the "good deals" and sell them before anyone else could.

Another example of this "programming" principle is when I was in my phase of building model sailboats. After having built three models I visited a hobby store to look for a challenging boat to build. They all seemed too small or too easy. In fact, the second two I had built were pretty easy compared to the first. When the salesperson asked if he could help me, I told him what I was looking for. He asked me how many I had built and I told him I had built three. He said, "Then you are still just a beginner, so I recommend some of these," pointing to all the easy boats I had rejected. I said, "No, I want something more like this," pointing to the one that I had built first, the *Cutty Sark*.

He quickly said, "No way, lady. I know people who have been building models for ten years who haven't tried the *Cutty Sark* yet. That's for masters." I told him that was the first boat I ever built and it was perfect. He told me that I was mistaken—that no one could build the *Cutty Sark* with full sails as his or her first boat. I knew that I was staring the end of my boat hobby right in the face. I left and never built another. Had I spoken with him, or apparently any other sailboat hobbyist, before I built my *Cutty Sark*, I never would have built it. Avoid limited thought!

I challenge you to know your own capabilities and limitations and never let anyone else program you to theirs. You are not "most people." You are you. If you always listen to what others say can or cannot be done, you will forever be falling short of expectations that you thought were reasonable and limiting your own capabilities to what "they" think is possible. Those concepts are based on averages or bad information. Do you want your target goal to be average? After you get advice, consider all aspects of it and do your own thinking. Do not assume everyone who offers advice is smarter or more knowledgeable than you are. Input from others is good, but it is only input. The output has to be *all* yours.

My Homes in Germany

My employment with the Department of Defense took me to an assignment in Europe. (Chapter Twelve elaborates on how this wonderful experience came about.)

My first apartment in Germany was in a pretty little town, Bärstadt, out in the foothills of the Taunus Mountains. It was such a lovely drive to and from my place of employment. The changing seasons were so beautiful in the hills that it was worth the terror of driving the curves and hills on the ice and snow of winter. Finding housing for an American at that time was difficult, so finding that first apartment was quite fortunate.

However, there was a young man in the neighborhood who seemed to be present everywhere we went. True, it was a very small village, but it did start to look a little odd. After about six months I began to get flowers and notes on my car. The notes were written in some very strange combination of English and German. I did understand enough German to interpret that he liked me and wanted me to meet him. The notes spoke of hiding places in the woods where there was "plenty of food" and he wanted me to go there with him and "bring the little girl." That did it—he was watching my daughter.

The letters were getting longer and longer and I would see him standing near my car in the mornings. I just ignored him, got in my car, and went to work. Then one day I saw him standing near my daughter's bus stop. She had to be at the bus stop about the time I needed to leave for work. That meant she was alone at the bus stop for five or ten minutes after I left. A change needed to occur.

When my landlady noticed who was leaving the notes, she got very concerned. She described him as the local "village idiot." Apparently he had been arrested a few times for stealing ladies' underwear off their clotheslines and his father was the leader of a radical political movement. As if this were not bad enough, I worked for a person who refused to allow me to adjust my working hours by fifteen minutes to be sure my daughter safely got on the school bus.

Obviously I needed to move, and quickly. So there I was, worrying about my daughter getting on the bus, needing to find a place to live in a time when fewer and fewer Germans were willing to rent to Americans, and not able to get time off from work to take care of the matter. People at the Housing Office for Americans were doing their best. All my friends put the word out that I was looking for a new apartment but most of them lived in government housing and did not have many contacts in the German communities.

After hearing of my situation, the Chief of Staff at our headquarters, who had personally offered me this assignment, was very concerned. He authorized everyone in our organization to give top priority to assisting us in finding a new apartment.

I was ready to give up. One morning as I sat in my car before entering work, I sent forth a prayer of complete relinquishment. "Dear God, I've done all I can do. This is no way to live. It is in your hands. Find me a home or I'll just return to the States."

About thirty minutes into the workday I was sitting at my desk, which faced directly down the central hall of our small office. At the end of that hall was a "secure" entry door because of our highly classified material. The buzzer on the door sounded which meant someone without a security clearance wanted access. Our administrative sergeant answered the door. I listened with disbelief as I heard the tall, slender young man at the door say, "I understand you have a lady working here with a young daughter who is looking for an apartment."

This young man was about to return to the United States and

he had been trying for over a month to find a good tenant for his landlords. They wanted a woman (or couple) with a young girl who could play with their daughter and help her learn English. He had given up and was on his way to the Housing Office to turn his apartment back in as being "available" when he made an unplanned stop to see a friend in the same building where I worked. He immediately heard about me and that was that.

The entire office helped me move into this absolutely incredible home. I had use of the garage, the whole third floor apartment, and the attic. The home backed into the hillside so I had access to a beautiful little backyard from my kitchen and my daughter's room. Straight up behind my yard were fruit orchards and on either side were grape vineyards. From my large front balcony I looked across to more hillside vineyards of the valley, and to my left I overlooked the cherry orchards through which I entered the town on a cobblestone road. Entering this village at cherry blossom time was incredible!

This is an excellent example of turning things completely over to God. You do what you can. As the Bible says, *"Faith without works is dead."* But when you leave the end results and the manner in which they work out in God's hands, you get results you could not possibly even dream to create for yourself. Had I kept pushing the situation, the Housing Office would have put me in the next tiny apartment that opened up and I would have gladly accepted.

We have all heard the expression, "Let go and let God," and I believe this is a great example of that dynamic.

San Antonio

From Europe I relocated to San Antonio, Texas. Following several moves, a failed marriage, and a friendly divorce, all I wanted was to simplify my life. I was running very late on my lunch hour one day when I drove by a condominium complex. I quickly turned in (while reminding myself that I did not have the time), zipped into the office, and was informed that one condo was available to rent. I looked. I loved it. It had a charming floor plan, was spacious, and was located only two traffic lights and one right turn from work.

Two years later, in June, I got a call from my daughter who was living near San Francisco. She announced she was getting married on July 9. She wanted to know if I would please come out over the Fourth of July weekend to meet him. Well, what would any Mom do? I made plans for the trip.

I got everything under control at work so I could get a few days off and made my travel arrangements. I was excited about shopping with my daughter for a wedding dress. A couple days before the trip I was walking up the steps to my front door thinking about how everything for the trip had fallen into place nicely. I reached for my doorknob and saw a typed notice taped to the door right at eye level. I pulled it off, thinking it was about the obligatory annual rent increase since the lease was about to expire. But the bold letters across the top caught my eye. It was an eviction notice! I had until the end of July. I laughed, thinking it was placed on the wrong door.

For the past three years I had been in a metaphysical study group. I lived on absolute faith, meditated, and had perpetual affirmations running in my head. It was working. I was happy and in control of events in my life. I understood the power of our words and thoughts and that all events are in perfect order. My response to this notice, after I read it three times and decided it really was for me, was throwing my hands in the air and saying, "You'll have to handle this, Lord. I don't have time." I proceeded to pack for my trip to meet my future son-in-law. I had no idea how long I would be gone—her plans were still a little vague. I refused to worry about it. There was no time.

Apparently, an investment company had purchased every condo occupied by a non-owner. Their process was to evict everyone as leases expired, fix them up, and then rent them out again. I failed to convince them that my apartment was in beautiful condition and that it was not logical for them to evict me, lose months of rent, and then take their chances on getting a quality renter. So I was definitely in the home-hunting business again.

I did not understand this. I truly loved this complex and loved the size and layout of my condo. Lottie, the lady downstairs, had become more family than friend. She had watched me coming and going while working sixteen-hour days and losing twenty-five pounds in one month because I did not have time to eat. Lottie began to meet me at whatever hour I got home and hand me a complete meal she had cooked earlier and kept warm. I believed with all my heart I belonged there. I could not even bring myself to look for another place, as the situation just seemed unreal. I was living as spiritually correct as I could and I did not understand how I could have created this. Falling back on faith and the creative power of affirmation, I kept repeating that good would come from this situation and I would have the perfect home at the perfect time.

On a pretty Sunday afternoon, after returning from San Francisco and with less than two weeks before my mandated move date, I decided to jump in my convertible and go apartment hunting. As I was on my way out, another downstairs neighbor saw me and started a conversation. I knew the only polite way to get going was to invite her along. I explained that I had to move by the end of the month and was on my way to check out a really nice area I had seen and she was welcome to join me.

As we headed out for our little adventure, I was rather amused that I would do this on a Sunday when nothing was open. I was even more amused that I would take someone with me whose company I enjoyed only for short periods of time. But Ella seldom had visitors or went out, so I knew she would welcome the opportunity. I think my own plan was more to *go for a spin* on a pretty day than it was to find an apartment.

We pulled in the drive of a small, secluded complex of condos. The entrance and its seclusion appealed to me but when I actually saw the office and buildings I was not sure it was for me. As expected, the office was closed and I was turning around to leave when an elderly lady living next to the office struck up a conversation with my Ella. She insisted we wait until she called one of her neighbors who could help us. I kept replying, "No, but thank you. I'll come back next week." But Ella kept saying, "Oh, let's wait. She says her neighbor can really help us." *Us?* At that point any response from me might have sounded rude so I agreed to wait. The kind, elderly lady invited us into her home to wait while she made the call. Guess who was accepting this invitation before I could say anything? That's right—Ella.

We sat there in a stranger's home for over forty minutes while she made attempts to reach her neighbor. I was initially under the impression that her neighbor could show us empty units in this particular complex. It soon became clear that her neighbor was a realtor and she was just trying to help her get a client. There were no units available at this location but she just knew her neighbor could help. This was a difficult enough situation without having a realtor trying to sell me a house instead of finding me an apartment. Worse yet, showing me a dozen apartments I would not want to live in. After about an hour of not being able to say no to this kind lady, her neighbor finally called and we spoke on the phone.

I do not like to be asked questions and I did not want to be in this situation where I had somehow lost control. As I answered all her questions and described what I wanted she said, "Oh, I know the perfect place for you—The Chesapeake." My chin almost hit the floor. That was where I currently lived. At least she understood my needs!

"I assure you there is nothing available. I checked with the office, called on every *For Sale* sign to see if they would rent, and asked every neighbor I saw. The investor who is evicting me purchased every vacant unit and all the rented units they could."

In spite of repeatedly thanking the realtor and telling her I did not think she could help me, she said she would check the MLS real estate listings and call me the next day. Agreeing was my way out of this situation. I jumped in my car, went home, and asked God to just "handle it." I had such a short time to move and I did not understand my own procrastination. I usually jump in and tackle any task.

The next morning the realtor actually did call me as she said she would. Surprisingly she said, "I found you a place." Appreciating her promptness I politely asked where. She said, "At The Chesapeake." I assured her this could not be but she told me the owners of the condo had just moved and they decided to rent it. It was listed in MLS that very morning. It was "on the market" less than an hour before she called me.

My current unit was wonderful but no rental is perfect. There were no curtains, only mini blinds. My balcony faced a wall behind which was a major road. I often imagined how great my furnishings would look on a light blue carpet and since I lived alone, I really wanted a security system. The new unit was the exact same floor plan and in a great location. It had beautiful, almost new light blue carpet with lovely drapes. It was an upstairs unit, which I always must have, and the balcony was literally in a treetop. Through the branches I could see the courtyard and swimming pool. The owners had also just recently installed a state-of-the-art security system. It was my same home in the same complex with every improvement I had thought of! I had been correct in my thinking—I was right where I belonged.

All my good works, faith, and intentions over the past few years had earned me an *upgrade*. Do not be quick to judge unexpected changes, even if they seem difficult. Remember that good can come from them. If you resist and struggle, the situation may have a poor result. Have faith, know it is pointing you in a good direction, and follow your instincts with a positive outlook. Could this be what is meant by *resist not evil?*

The universal laws of creation were at work for me each time I searched for a home. I gave up the struggle. In the early years I took this as simple answered prayers. Later I realized that the prayers were answered because of my faith and my affirmative statements regarding what I wanted. I had created with my thoughts and desires. Never once did I intend that "any old place would do." Each time I made up my mind to get something ideal. I had intention, with emotion behind it and my desires never adversely affected anyone else. The difference between knowingly using these principles and using them unconsciously is that you worry a whole lot less while in a transition. Trust is very calming.

I could have easily been drawn into negativity and used thoughts and words like, "I'll never find a place I like," or "I'll never be able to afford what I want." In such a case I would have found and settled for much less. I have seldom succumbed to negativity, but I have missed many chances to boldly ask for and expect more—from myself, from others, and from God. I had obviously noticed that every time I really made up my mind to do something, or to have something, that it happened. Understanding the laws of cause and effect and how all that we think, say, and do is *causing* an *effect* is magic. It is your own personal magic wand—have faith and use it.

Dallas

A few years later when I took a job in Dallas, I needed to find an apartment very quickly. By some interesting *coincidences*, I found the perfect complex. I was hoping to put off signing a lease for a short time because Mercury was retrograde. (For those of you with an interest in astrology, you know that you do not want to sign contracts or make important decisions when Mercury is retrograde because it will end up changed in some way or be reversed.)

As the Universe would have it, I got word that an old friend was going to be in Dallas on a certain date. That date, as I recall was about four days before Mercury went direct. My options were to take the apartment and get my things up to Dallas while the pesky little planet was still retrograde or miss seeing my friend for what could have been several more years.

Those retrograde energies are there for a reason. I found it interesting that a situation was, for a lack of better terms, *forcing* me to sign my lease under those energies. Trusting the Universe and the whole situation, I signed the lease, my friend visited, and we had a great time.

After being in my apartment for less than a week (right after Mercury went direct), I knew I could not stay there. Not only was the apartment NOT on the top floor (which they said it was), the person upstairs worked out with heavy equipment and weights in the middle of the night. He may have been good at lifting them, but he was not gentle at setting them down.

Some of the buildings in the complex had three floors and some had four floors. A new leasing agent had mistakenly given me a third-floor apartment that she believed was on the top floor. They had no top floor units available, so in an attempt to correct the situation in time for all my stored belongings to arrive from San Antonio, the manager emptied out one of their furnished executive suites. It was in a premium location with a great view. It had upgraded paint and cabinets and the manager offered to put in new carpet for me. It became a charming home and I loved living there.

Had circumstances not guided me to sign a contract while Mercury was retrograde, I would not have had those energies of change working with me and I might have been stuck in a difficult living condition. For sure, I would not have had that premium unit had management not been correcting a mistake. And I would never have met my neighbor, Ann, who is still a friend today. When unusual circumstances seem to lead you, follow. If you are living a well-intentioned life, the Universe will very cleverly work things out for you.

My Current Home

I have been in my current home for over eight years. It is in a terrific location in Phoenix, Arizona, and I found it while zigzagging through unfamiliar streets to avoid a traffic jam. On the day I went to sign the papers, I was a bit nervous. I was using every penny I had for the down payment. At the last minute I was informed of an appraisal fee and inspection fee that amounted to about five hundred dollars. I did not have the extra money, but I really believed this to be a good decision; so there I was on my way to buy a house.

While waiting at a red light just a block before the sales office, I began to feel the weight of such a large commitment at this particular time. On the green light I drove through the intersection and whispered a prayer, "God, I'm going to do this. You will just have to come up with five hundred dollars for me."

Seconds later I was hit from behind by a vehicle containing four young boys who were not totally focused on the traffic. I called the sales office and told them I had had an accident just a half of a block away and I would be there as soon as a policeman took a report. I eventually got there, signed the papers, and that was that.

The next day I received a call from the other car owner's insurance company and I was asked if I could come to the office and let the claims adjuster look at my car. All the accident had done was leave a big smudge spot on my bumper. I was actually not very concerned about it but nonetheless, I had a right to have it corrected.

The insurance agent looked at the damage and said it really couldn't be corrected so they would no doubt have to replace the bumper. He asked me if I would accept a check for five hundred dollars and take care of the issue myself. Easy decision! I agreed, collected the five hundred dollars, and lived with the smudge on my rear bumper as long as I owned the car.

Chapter Seven

Contact from the Other Side

In July of 1980 I returned to the United States after living and working in Europe. Texas took a little getting used to after Europe, but I grew to love the great state, especially the city of San Antonio. By fall I settled into a new job working for the commander of a training organization on a local Air Force base. I thoroughly enjoyed the organization and my closest associates who consisted of the commander and his executive officer (EO). By spring we had melded into a great team.

The EO and I shared a small office just off a main hallway. In May, the doorway from that hall into the office became a point of intrigue and distraction for me. With increasing regularity this doorway was a portal for a message from the other side.

Several times each day when my vision was cast in the direction of the doorway, I saw the image of Bob, a man I had known and cared for while living in Europe. Although this image was quite vivid, it was seen with my mind, not with my physical eyes. The image was always the same and though it was a still image, his position implied movement, as if he were walking through the door toward me.

Since moving back to the States, I had missed talking with Bob and often wondered how he was doing with his new assignment in Central America. This recurring image of him began to heighten my concern. I had no idea why this was happening or what it meant. I thought perhaps it was something telepathic, which meant he was also thinking of me. Honestly, there were times when it frightened me. It would not go away.

One unusually slow day at the office, our commander returned from a morning meeting across town and stopped just inside the doorway to talk about his meeting. This put the doorway right in my line of sight and the image of Bob was there the entire time. After sharing his thoughts, the commander walked on in with a big smile on his face and showed the EO and me a big book he had brought back with him.

The commander was funny, pleasant, friendly, good at his job, and loved his Air Force career in the best possible way. He loved his fellow officers and the stories they all shared. He placed the book on the EO's desk and said, "This is a book of champagne flights from Colonel Johnson's fighter squadron. I thought you guys might find it interesting."

I was not sure why I did what I did next, but I jumped up, grabbed the book, sat in the chair by the EO's desk and said, "I know someone in this book." I couldn't believe the words as I heard them come out of my mouth. Yet I sat there, turning the pages quickly and with purpose. Suddenly, there it was—a photo of Bob (whom I could still see standing in the doorway) after his champagne flight.

A "champagne flight" was a ride in a fighter jet given to pilots who had been held in Vietnam as prisoners of war. Following their release in 1973, a qualified pilot from their former squadrons took each of them up for a ride and they opened a bottle of champagne when they landed. My friend had been a POW for six and a half years after his jet was shot down.

My only verbal response to finding the photograph was,

"There he is." I placed the book back on the EO's desk and went back to mine. I just sat there numb. How did I know he was in the book? What was going on? I pulled my calendar toward me from the front edge of my desk. I must have thought (or hoped) that looking at my schedule would bring me back into the reality of the day. I found myself staring at today's date and then in disbelief I realized that this very day was his birthday.

That did it! I just had to talk to him. As far as I knew, Bob was already on his next foreign assignment but there was a chance he was still in Washington at the language school in preparation. I called the military locator and they said there was no one by that name on active duty. I called several times that week hoping for a different answer. Bob had been so looking forward to this assignment that I felt there was no way he would retire. However, I eventually called back and asked them to check their retired list. After confirming he was not on either list, an uneasy feeling would not allow me to consider a third option. I immediately convinced myself I had done all that could be done to reach him and forced the whole situation from my mind.

A couple of months later I had an opportunity to reassign to an organization on another base in the area. I was reluctant to leave my current position, but felt it was the right thing to do. One day in late September I had a sudden need to find out exactly what had happened to my friend. It came from nowhere.

I grabbed the phone and dialed the locator once more. Speaking very quickly I explained how I had checked the active duty and retired lists and asked her if there was another list she could check. She told me she had a directory of deceased officers that she could check but they were not allowed to give that information out over the phone. Well, I am not easily denied when I have made up my mind to something and I was not getting off the phone without my answer. I convinced her I would be quite fine and she reluctantly agreed to check the list for me. Some time later she came back to the phone and announced, "Yes, your friend is on the list . . ." That was all I heard. I fell out of my chair on to the floor. My mind went numb, my hearing was affected, and my muscles would hardly work. It seemed like forever, but I made my way back up to my desk and picked up the telephone receiver, which was hanging off the end of the desk. I put the receiver to my ear and said, "Are you still there?" Bless her heart, she was.

I am not exactly sure what I said to her, but she very compassionately said, "Now I know why they say *never* give out this type of information on the phone. I'm very sorry. I will put all the details in a letter and send it to you."

For the next several days, while waiting on the letter, my mind was consumed by thoughts of his image appearing so persistently in the doorway and a seven-year-old photograph of a man I knew in Europe finding its way to my desk from across town in San Antonio on his birthday. In a few days I did receive the letter and I read it over and over. It was somewhat clinical and to the point. In short, he had had a sudden heart attack. On what was probably the tenth reading, I realized that the letter had reached me on the first anniversary of his death and it had been just a year ago that his image began presenting itself so strongly.

About four years later I met Karen Fletcher, a truly gifted psychic and medium, and we became good friends. One day she asked me if I knew a man by a particular name. She made several attempts with slight variations of a name. I was thinking of first names so it did not seem familiar. Then she said, "He's showing me a parachute and he's wrapping it around you as you walk down the street to keep you warm. It seems he did this to you when he was still here. The fact that he is using a parachute is supposed to mean something." Suddenly I got it. The name she was attempting to relate was one letter off from Bob's last name. He had parachuted out of his aircraft and he used to wrap his coat around me on cool evenings in Germany when we would walk to a restaurant for dinner.

His message, sent through my friend, was that he would always be there watching out for me. One of the last things Bob ever said to me when he was alive was that he felt as if he "owed" me. He said no one had ever put so much effort into caring for him. He appreciated the help I gave him through some serious injuries and surgery and was truly grateful.

Approximately one year after that message was delivered through Karen, I was in a situation with many important decisions to be made. I found myself wishing that Bob were there—I just knew he would have some wise and simple guidance. I had recently accepted a better position and was working at yet another government installation. As I got to work this particular soul-searching morning, I was informed that the commander wanted all employees in his office in ten minutes. Ten minutes later I was busy on an important phone call so my supervisor instructed me to complete the conversation and he would explain my lateness.

Only a few minutes later I joined everyone in the commander's office. He had an important announcement to make and had decided to wait until I arrived. He welcomed me and I looked around for an inconspicuous place to sit or stand. Most people were standing around the perimeter of the room, however, two of the girls had taken the couch and saved me a seat right in the middle. I walked over, sat down, and right in front of me was an album. A strange, familiar feeling came over me. Following the commander's announcement, I opened the book and this time slowly turned the pages. Yes, I eventually came to the same photograph of a champagne flight I had seen several years earlier. Bob was just letting me know he was still around, I guess.

When I completed what I thought was my final draft of this book, this is where this chapter ended. However, I was provided one more exciting demonstration of the power that our friends and loved ones on the other side have to contact and influence us. I felt compelled to add an update.

In early December 2005, I made plans to visit my life-long friends, Joyce and Bruce, in Germany. Our three lives have intertwined since kindergarten and Joyce is also a distant cousin.

Not only did we go through school together, but when I lived in Wiesbaden, Germany, they were not far away in Stuttgart. Now they frequently visit their grown daughters who live in Tucson not far from me. We also attend our high school class reunions every five years.

Joyce had a mild health scare and she was on extended leave through the holidays. She suggested it was a good time for me to visit. She had the time and she knew I loved Germany at Christmas. I was also concerned for her well being so I agreed.

Since I would be missing the holidays at home, I had many things to do before leaving. Having lunch with my friend, Irene was one of them.

Several days before meeting with Irene, I received an e-mail from my favorite independent bookstore in Tempe, Arizona, Changing Hands. They were posting a notice that they had a limited number of autographed copies of a book by Paul McCartney. The books had gone on sale at eight o'clock that morning and it was now noon. Always the optimist, I called but was informed they had sold out about thirty minutes earlier. I decided to drive over to the bookstore in person and ask again. Perhaps someone had called and cancelled a "hold" on one of the copies. Perhaps they had one more under the counter they had covered up and forgotten about. Being used to miracles here and there, I arrived and asked for a copy of the Paul McCartney book. Disappointed at the answer, I decided to stay and look around anyway.

Almost immediately I came across a book titled *My Hero*. It was a small book with a pretty blue cover and an interesting title so I looked through it. It was a collection of essays by famous people (who are often considered inspirational themselves) as to who inspired them. The essays were all signed by their well-known authors. This was great! My friend Irene is a handwriting expert and she enjoys looking at signatures of public figures. This was the perfect Christmas gift for her.

A day or so later, I saw the book lying on my dining room table and decided to look through it a little more closely. I noticed there was a section by Senator John McCain of Arizona. I have seen several programs on Senator McCain's military experience and his time as a POW in Vietnam. On occasion I would wonder if there was any chance he knew Bob. Being very familiar with Senator McCain, I only briefly skimmed over his bio and hurried to his narrative to see whom he considered his hero. The first sentence began, "A friend of mine, Bob Craner, once told me a story . . ." I had just received one more contact from my friend and my curiosity of their knowing each other was satisfied. By the way, they shared Ted Williams as their hero.

I had lunch with Irene, showed her the book, and she loved it. Then I told her the story and said the book was now too special to give away, but I would get her another one when I returned from Germany. When I got back I tried to do just that. The clerk at the bookstore told me they had no record of carrying that book, but they could order it. Interesting, don't you think?

I believe we all have many loved ones on the other side who do their best to guide us and let us know they are close. They are only the sender of images or signs. Every sender needs a receiver. Busy, angry or negative energy of any sort does not make a good receiver. Neither does being overly focused on the details of tomorrow or next week allow you to notice such signs today. Put effort into calming your mental energies and learn to be completely aware of the present. That is where your life is. That is the only place anything can happen.

Chapter Eight

Dreams, Visions, and Visitations

About Dreams

We are conditioned from early childhood that our dreams are not real. Most of us can remember hearing, or saying, "It was only a dream." I must admit that it is not a good idea to tell a small child his bad dream was probably a true experience which happened a long, long time ago when he or she was another person. But I would like to see parents of young children find a way to make them feel safe and unafraid without completely imbedding the notion that dreams are meaningless.

Dreams are an area of great interest and concern to many. As more and more people have become spiritually astute, the subject of dream interpretation has received more attention. I have always given a great amount of thought to dreams; they have been plentiful and very seldom meaningless.

For me, some dreams seem to be just a buildup and release of mental activity, much like static electricity producing a spark. Those dreams feel pretty silly when we wake up. I have always referred to these as *clutter dreams*. They just release a lot of clutter from your mind. On the days following these *clutter dreams* you will probably notice that you have a lot more mental energy.

Then there are what I call *message dreams*. Those are dreams that do not fade so quickly. They seem very real and make you wonder about their meaning. The *clutter dreams* may make you wonder why on earth you would dream such a thing, but the *message dreams* leave a haunting curiosity; you want to figure them out and you remember them for much longer. You should always write these dreams down. If you are diligent enough to record such dreams in a journal, they will seem almost as real when you read them back as they did when you woke up.

Anyone wishing to make sense out of dream information must keep a written record. It is a good idea to keep a journal right by the bed and record the dreams as soon as you wake up. How many times have you had a dream so vivid that you lie awake thinking about it for a long time, thinking how you could never forget it? Yet so often it is gone by morning or within minutes after waking. Sometimes the meanings of my dreams are quite clear and other times I can sense that there is another message I am not seeing. Sharing dreams with a group of people who are spiritual minded can bring insight. If you would like to learn more about dreams, I strongly recommend studying books containing Edgar Cayce's material on dreams.

In the meantime, I suggest taking the following steps:
- Record your dreams. Keep a pad and pencil by the bed and write your dreams down to be read later.
- Categorize the dream as a clutter dream, message dream or vision (discussed later). This should be your first impression that can be adjusted later.
- List key elements in the dream and what they mean to you. Details are important.
- Leave enough room to write down your later impressions.
- Occasionally read over your dream journal. New impressions might come to you. Events may have

transpired since the dream that will help give it meaning.

Here is an example of how this might go: Let's say you have a dream where you and your sister are riding in a raft in very rough water. Each wave tosses your raft into the air only to fall back to the water in time for the next wave to repeat the turbulence. Your sister is riding along with a smile as if it were a sailboat on a glassy lake. You are frightened and want it to stop, but you say nothing. You also notice that your hair is very red in this dream, which is not your normal color.

Key elements of this dream might be sister, raft, water, fear, and red hair. I think the confined space of the raft with you and your sister would indicate that it only involved the two of you, therefore, your relationship. Water typically represents emotions and red hair typically represents anger. It would seem that being emotionally tossed about in relation to your sister has caused you some anger. She was undisturbed which might indicate that she was either enjoying the part that tossed you about and made you angry or she was totally unaware of any of your emotional issues. Either way, you and your sister had two different perceptions of your emotional issues.

Of course this dream could have totally different meanings for different people. What if you and your sister had been caught out in a raft when you were young? This would entirely change the approach to the dream. In that case, perhaps you are still angry that no one had understood your fear and maybe you should explain it to whoever was involved at the time.

Tragedy Avoided Through Dreams

Dreams can be an incredible source of information. It is possible to deliberately channel information through your dreams—simply ask for information to come to you in a dream. You must have faith that the answer will come and you must be prepared for what comes through. As dreams are so often difficult to interpret, ask for clarity.

At my annual Association for Research and Enlightenment (A.R.E.) retreat held sometime in the mid 1990s, our main topic was dreams. Our speaker, John Van Auken, gave us an assignment to ask for an answer through our dreams to an important matter in our lives. We were to share the results the next day. I climbed into my upper bunk that night in one of the grand stone buildings of this beautiful retreat in the Texas hill country. I tried and tried to think of a question but one never came. I was amused because I always had one phase or another of my life in some state of flux or change and I always needed an answer to something. Yet at this particular time I seemed to need nothing. So, trusting the Universe to always guide me, I made a simple prayer asking the Universe to provide me with whatever information I should know, even though I was not aware of the need. After this prayerful thought I fell asleep with a cool fall breeze blowing through the window and across my bunk.

I woke up a short time later, startled by a clear and profound dream. In spite of my belief in this process and my attachment to this very special place, I thought the Universe had made a big mistake. I had the *wrong* dream. Or maybe I just didn't like it. The dream went like this:

> I was up in the air looking down on a rural Texas highway. I hovered high above this road and just ahead I saw flashing emergency vehicle lights. There were two cars in the ditch with several police and ambulance vehicles surrounding them. As I focused on the white car that was off the road, I had what I refer to as a "knowing." I knew that I was looking down on my friend Laura's white car that we had driven to this retreat. A familiar feeling came to me, and I understood completely what I was seeing. Laura was in the car and they were trying to help her. No one was trying to help me. I had died and my spirit was hovering over the area just as it had in the hospital over twenty-five years earlier. That is when I woke up.

Not liking the dream and not thinking it was appropriate to what I was asking or what our assignment was, I dismissed it. Again I prayed to be provided with whatever information I might need at this particular time. I fell asleep quickly. Again, after what seemed like a short period of time, I awoke. I was even more startled than the first time; I'd had the same identical dream! Every sight, thought, and feeling was exactly the same with even the same pace and timing. The only exception was that visually, the entire dream was shifted slightly to the right. Imagine looking at a dream through a camera lens, then moving the camera slightly to the left, shifting all the images in view to your right. Otherwise, the two dreams were identical.

There was no doubt at this point that I had the right dream and I knew exactly what it meant. That slight shift to the right made it very clear to me. The dream seemed to say, "I am telling you what you asked for — *again.*" That slight shift to the right was a strong statement of deliberateness on the part of the Universe. I got the point.

Car accidents happen only because two cars try to occupy the same space at the same time. I knew what I needed to do but I said nothing to Laura. The next morning we had our final meeting in which many people shared answers they had received in dreams and what they meant to their current situation. I said nothing. I was well aware of the importance of timing and all I had to do was quietly alter the timing of when we would be on that road. Our plan was to leave at one o'clock that day. The accident that was revealed to me had to have been based on our planned time of departure. I did not take this lightly and I kept the dream foremost in my thoughts all morning. I asked for one more sign. I asked for a sign to confirm that all I had to do was alter the time sequence of events.

After our last meeting we had our healing meditation on the riverbank. This was always the last event of the program and was held just before lunch after which we would all leave. Laura and I went to the dining hall for lunch and to say our goodbyes. Then it was off to the bunkhouse to pack up. Our hearts and spirits were in a good place as we packed and shared memories of the retreat with our bunkmates. We picked up our final pieces of baggage and headed to the car. As I placed the last piece in the trunk, Laura and I looked at each other and sighed our regret that this wonderful weekend was over. I closed the trunk of Laura's car and asked, "Laura, what time is it?" She looked at her watch and said with amazement, "It is *exactly* one o'clock. We are perfectly on schedule."

That was my sign. I said, "Laura. We need to talk." I told her about my dream and it scared her to death. I said, "Laura, the point is that there is nothing to be afraid of. All we have to do is alter our timing. Our car just can't be in *that* place at *that* time. We have probably done so just by having this conversation, but let's take one more walk down to the river and sit on the dock in the sun for a while." We enjoyed lingering and giving thanks for this guidance and we finally left a little before two o'clock. Our return to Dallas was fun and uneventful.

It is important to understand the potential of dreams. But there is no need to be obsessed with finding an exact meaning for every little dream. However, with a heightened awareness there will be some dreams to which you give extra thought. Keep your journal, read it once in a while, ask for understanding, and have faith you will grow to use your dreams as guides. Even if you do not consciously get the precise message, the subconscious is ever connecting us to our higher self and translating messages to our "gut instincts."

My Oregon Dream

While living in Phoenix I have often considered the idea of moving to Oregon. The pros and cons of such a move were too equally weighted to make a decision. It seemed worthy of soliciting an answer in a dream.

As I tried to settle in for some sleep on a hot August night, I was overly bothered by the fact that I had no real sense of *where to live next*. In Europe I wanted to go to San Antonio and I did. From San Antonio I wanted to go to Dallas and I did. From Dallas I wanted to move to Phoenix and I did. But I was now in a state of transition with no definite idea where I might really be happy. I was truly yearning for that place I would never want to leave.

I certainly had options. I could go to Oregon to be near my daughter and grandson. A part of me thought it would be great to move back to my hometown to be near my parents and other family members. A big part of me just plain missed Texas. Yet none compelled me to a decision.

Through my medium friend, Karen Fletcher, my grandfather had once let me know that he would try to communicate with me through my dreams. I lay in bed mentally speaking to my grandfather. I explained that I needed clarity through a dream as to where I should go — where I would be happy. It could be one of my preferences or a place I had never been.

I explained to Grandpa that as much as I would love to see his face and hear him laugh, I did not think it would be a good idea if *he* came to me in the dream. I wanted very clear guidance and I was concerned that if he were in my dream it could be explained as my missing him and having thought about him before falling asleep. Whatever it took, I wanted unquestionable guidance — something I would not second-guess or wonder about, and I trusted it to come.

Somewhere in the very early morning hours I awoke a couple of times after very brief and fuzzy dreams. Although I could not remember them, they felt special and intense. I really felt as if my answer was trying to come through. With great anticipation I quickly fell back to sleep. The next time I awoke, I just lay there motionless and I did not open my eyes. I wanted to stay with the thoughts and emotions of the incredible gift I had received in my dream. This was a dream, vision, and visitation all in one.

It began with my standing at the edge of a road. I was looking down toward the ground and I was standing on small, round, black stones. I remember thinking it was interesting that they were black. They were quite beautiful. This stone-covered area was along the shoulder of the road and it was wide enough to accommodate two or three cars. As I looked up to my left side, the road trailed off quickly due to a sharp left curve. I was surrounded by pine trees that lined the road and the air was notably sweet and fresh.

Next I noticed a lady sitting in a rocking chair several yards beyond the black stones in a grassy clearing. I was no longer standing on the ground — I was viewing her from slightly higher and farther away. I came closer to her. I could see her face and it was Angela Lansbury, the actress. She was sitting in a rocking chair with a blanket over her knees. Her face was radiant as she smiled at me, and she embodied the essence of calm, joy, contentment, love, poise, peace, and lightness of thought and body. She sat erect, yet relaxed. Her smile was more than loving — it was approving. That smile of approval ran through my being, completely validating my life.

In a moment I was back in my original position on the black stones. My attention was directed to the guardrail that separated the stone-covered area from the grassy clearing where Angela Lansbury sat. Beyond the clearing were more pine trees.

I began to hear beautiful, soft music coming from deep inside the guardrail. My focus was brought to an area in the center of the guardrail at its left end, just before it bent to the ground. I was amazed and puzzled so I looked questioningly toward Angela. I was again taken aback by her presence, her wise and comforting smile, and a slight nod to acknowledge the melodic voices. Looking back to the guardrail, I could see, hear, and feel the music. I leaned closer to the celestial sounds then sat down in my own rocking chair that had just appeared behind me. It was impossible to consume these wondrously moving sounds and remain standing. It was penetrating and overwhelming. It sounded as if a thousand voices were blended as one, yet it was possible to also hear each of the thousand voices. For a while I was hearing only sweet, wordless changes in tones and then came the very clear and distinct words "Oregon Trees" harmonized into the melody. "Oregon Trees" came out in four notes that were even more lovely than the previous sounds.

After the singing of "Oregon Trees" the music went back to inspiring melodic tones. Still in my rocker I looked back down the road with all its surrounding trees. Once more I heard the musical words of "Oregon Trees." I absorbed these sounds as if I were porous. I sat looking down the road and felt my self-awareness altering. I realized then that I was much older and that looking back the road represented looking back over a long period of time. I had a sense of having spent many years there and I was extremely content with all I had experienced.

I rested my head on the back of the rocker and closed my eyes and felt immensely content.

For a third time my beautiful voices sang "Or-e-gon Trees." With this, tears of joy trickled down my face and I was overwhelmed with satisfaction. I sat there, eyes closed, absorbing the sounds. For the first time I understood the true definition of "glorious."

When I woke up, I knew I had my answer. I lay there with my eyes closed, trying not to wake up too fast. I wanted to stay close to those sounds and feelings as long as I could.

When you hear heavenly voices singing "*Oregon* Trees" from a *guard*rail, and you are being watched over by *Angel*a Lansbury, and are left with a feeling of a *life well spent,* it does not take great interpretive skills to realize my Guardian Angel was telling me I would be happy in Oregon and that I would realize my quest for contentment as she watched over me.

I'm not sure when or how, but it looks like Oregon is definitely in my future.

Good job, Grandpa!

About Visions

Visions can come during deep meditation, while you are completely awake, or they can come to you in a dream. There are some people who have visions spontaneously or on command. But most ordinary people, like myself, have them during meditation or in dreams. It is important to train yourself in recognizing the differences between your *message dreams* and *visions*. This may be a little like splitting a hair, but I think it is an important hair to split. I believe the *message dreams* bring forth knowledge from past lives, from collective consciousness, from angels, or from Grandma who is on the other side. I believe *Visions* come from God. Keep in mind this is my terminology based on my impressions from my experiences. However, this should provide a frame of reference and guidance as you proceed along your own personal journey.

If you have a vision you will know it. It will seem profoundly different. You will never forget anything about it, even if you do not write it down. You will be able to recall every detail twenty years later. Neither the image nor the message it brings will fade in the slightest. The message may be profound guidance on an important decision or it may simply leave you with a feeling of comfort and a sense of being watched over. You will know absolutely that it is coming from the Source. "Believers" will feel blessed. "Non-believers" will know beyond a doubt that they have had an unexplainable experience and they will always be looking for an explanation that will not come. They may adopt some explanation just because they need one, but it will never offer them complete satisfaction.

My Favorite Vision

One of my most powerful and empowering *visions* happened when I was in a guided meditation. Meditation exercises can be self-guided or guided by another person leading a group. Either way, the events that you will image in your mind are being directed. For example, the leader may start, "You are walking through a field of long green grass with a slight breeze on your face. You are walking toward a gentle, narrow stream and you can hear the water babbling over rocks as you move toward the stream."

As you create these guided images in your mind, this is a *visualization*. What can happen is that the *visualization* turns into a *vision*, which is like watching a video—you now have no control over what is being seen. Images play out and you are simply the observer.

My friend Bonnie once came to Phoenix to visit and as a "thank you" for showing her around, she generously treated both of us to a spa day at the city's finest resort. We had a fine day being pampered and getting a little sun. One of the treatment options at the spa was a meditation session in their marvelous meditation room. This room was specifically designed for meditation and it was an incredibly peaceful little spot. It was full of plants; it had a waterfall and skylights. There were reclining chairs of perfect size and contour placed spaciously among the plants, and even the size of the room was perfect.

The energy in the room was peaceful and very inviting of Spirit. The icing on the cake was the voice of the lady leading the meditation. It was soft and gentle without sounding contrived. It seemed to flow seamlessly into the air like an audible mist that blended with the air, the music and my body. I was glad we were there.

As the meditation began, it was very easy to image what the leader was saying. With her guidance, I clearly visualized myself walking along a stream and I came upon a waterfall. By the time I was at the waterfall, I had trouble staying with the guide. Instead, my mind wanted to wander. I kept forcing it back to the sound of her voice. Then, as I stood looking up at a large, wide waterfall, everything changed. I no longer heard the guide and I was only an observer as I stood across the stream watching this beautiful creation of nature.

I watched this massive wall of white falling water and an image began to form out of it. Out of the white water came a huge white bird. As it formed from the falls, it moved toward me with open wings and wrapped me up and flew away. I felt the wings enfold me and fly away, yet I remained in my same position and watched the bird flying upward through the sky with me wrapped in its arms—much as a mother would carry a small infant. I stood there marveling at the sight and was moved by the experience. As I watched, the bird transformed. Its wings and tail became the draping sleeves and trailing skirt of a white robe. The head of the bird had become a familiar face and there I was watching myself fly away in the arms of Christ. The overwhelming sense of love and acceptance was consuming. Then my conscious position within the vision changed. I went from standing across the stream as an observer to feeling myself securely in His arms, moving through what felt like time, not space.

After this I started being aware of something bumping my leg and voices that sounded far away. The meditation leader was tapping my leg and others in the group were softly calling my name. Apparently the meditation had ended and I did not respond. Everyone in the room had become quite concerned. My eyes opened and I slowly became aware of my surroundings. Tears were streaming from my eyes and apparently had been for a while as the front of my shirt was wet from tears. Tears continued to flow easily as I shared my experience with them. This *vision* has been a treasure for me. Pure love cannot be described in this dimension.

Similar incidents can happen within a dream. The dream will seem to be interrupted with this video-like episode just as my meditation was interrupted. It will seem more important than anything going on in the dream and you will pay attention to it, almost as if you were casually watching television and an important news bulletin had come on. In these cases you will forget what was interrupted but clearly remember the interruption.

Visitations

Visitations are unique and rare for most of us, but I cannot help believing that we have a lot more *visitations* than we actually notice. Two possible examples of visitations are my Christmas Angel and the subsequent insurance agent of Chapter Four. Another may be the mobile home salesperson who was there for my one sale then moved on. Many people have had *visitations* by the spirit of a loved one.

Laura and I had a *visitation* one day at lunch. Laura, my friend who attended the retreat on dreams with me, was a vendor for one of my projects at work so we often discussed business over lunch. Since we were such good friends, lunch was a comfortable way for us to get a lot accomplished. I told Laura I was going to stop by the restroom on my way out and she decided to join me.

We paid our check and walked across the small lobby area to an open doorway marked "Restrooms." As we approached this doorway we saw a stocky, dark-haired gentleman walking by from our left to our right. We waited for him to pass then entered the short hallway that went just a short way to the right and then turned left to the restrooms. The door to the men's room was on our immediate left. The gentleman, now directly in front of us, opened the door slightly then backed out and went the several steps to the end of that hall to the ladies' room door, opened it just enough to walk in and let it close behind him.

Laura and I were watching in disbelief. We waited a moment, assuming he would just pop right back out realizing his mistake. When he did not come out, we just laughed, shrugged our shoulders and proceeded through the door ourselves. He was nowhere in sight. We quickly looked at each other very uncomfortably. It was a tiny space. There was a very small-framed lady standing at a mirror fixing her hair who seemed concerned that we were just looking around. Without a word we looked in the two empty stalls and waited for the only other person to exit the third stall—a very tall and slender lady. When they left the room Laura and I were the only ones there.

Still having said not a word to each other, Laura and I walked out to her car to return to work. Laura started the car and just as she started to back out she asked, "Are we going to talk about what just happened in there?"

I said, "Yes." She shut off the car and we both burst out laughing. We sat there and analyzed the situation for some time.

The man had been just inches from us. We had seen him first walking the entry hallway from left to right but on the way out we noticed there was no place on the left for him to be coming "from." There was just a wall at the end of the hall. We had almost bumped into him when he first started to enter the men's room then backed out. We both recalled every detail of what happened and his physical description identically. We had both seen him slip into the ladies' room. We had entered the restroom just seconds behind him. We both agreed there had been no time for him to be more than three or four steps in front of us.

Both ladies in the restroom were professionally dressed and obviously there for business lunches. The lady at the mirror had things from her purse spread all over the counter as if she had been there a few minutes. She obviously had not seen anyone.

Our discussion just went in circles and we had no idea what to make of it except that we had both just seen a man who had disappeared.

In retrospect there are only a couple of things I could add to this. It's as clear in my mind as if it had happened yesterday. There was no time at which either of us saw his face or even the side of his face. But we could describe the back of his head perfectly. Also, he was a rather hefty man, yet he had opened the door only about ten or twelve inches wide, slipped in, and let the door close quickly behind him. I actually remember wondering at the time how he had slipped in there so easily.

Do I have an afterthought or a possible meaning for this one?

No. I will wonder on it forever. Laura and I laughed about it frequently in the months that followed.

Laura later tried to tell another person about this disappearing act but it did not go very well. I said, "Laura, you just had your first lesson about keeping unusual experiences to yourself. People will think you are nuts!" Almost every time Laura and I were together, incredible things happened. Perhaps Laura and I were each at a critical point for expanding our consciousness from *believing* to *knowing* and we provided validation for each other that extraordinary, even unbelievable events are real.

Nonetheless, it was great fun.

Chapter Nine
The Right Books Will Find You

Once you make a conscious decision to align your life with spiritual concepts, you will be continually amazed at how information comes to you — especially through books.

You might be in line to buy a movie ticket when the person beside you says, "I just finished this book and I always pass my books on. Would you like this one?" You might take it only to be polite but out of curiosity you read it and find an answer to a burning question. Only the Universe knew where your best answer was hiding and how to get it to you.

On a restless night you might stay up unusually late and click through the television channels. You hear a writer promoting a book that is about the very subject on which you need information.

Then again, you could be in a bookstore browsing the cookbook section when you find a misplaced book on a specific health issue that has been bothering you. If this happens to you — buy the book!

As a teenager, two books came into my life. One was Jean

Dixon's *The Gift of Prophecy* and the other was *Many Mansions*, a book about the work of Edgar Cayce. Reading books was not an activity in my childhood home nor was it encouraged. I cherished having these books and did not care what they were about. I read them with great interest. I thought it unusual that only two books found their way to me and they happened to be of the same nature.

Later, at age thirty-five, while moving into my new apartment, I once again came across the book *Many Mansions*. Where had it been all these years? I had moved at least eight times since I had first read it, yet it had never surfaced. Honestly, I never knew where it came from the first time. Reading it again was more thought provoking than before. It no longer read as the interesting experiences of someone who lived before my time; rather, it read as material that could help me make sense out of my life today. What if I had past lives and what if they directly contributed to my life's experiences? It also suggested solutions and corrective actions. Not knowing anyone who was interested in this type of material or where to go for more answers, the book ultimately went back into a box where it would wait until I was even more open to its knowledge.

About three years later I was selling herbs from my home in addition to my regular employment. One of my clients called and said she would like to stop by and give me some information. I was a little busy, but she was being so nice I told her to come on by. She made a small herb purchase, then gave me some information about an Association for Research and Enlightenment (A.R.E.) meeting. She explained that this was an organization based on Edgar Cayce's material. (There was Edgar Cayce again!)

I grew more interested as the days passed by and the date for the meeting drew close. The location of the meeting was nearby and it should not have taken me more than ten or fifteen minutes to get there. But the directions on the map were not quite clear and the site of the meeting was not externally marked. I spent two hours finding the right building and the right room where the meeting was being held. I detest being late and it is very unlike me to attend anything where I cannot be on time. I arrived as the speaker was offering closing remarks and thanking everyone for attending.

I quietly sat at the rear of the small gathering beside a lady named Miriam. She was kind enough to tell me briefly about A.R.E. and Edgar Cayce. I told her I was not sure why I came, but that I seemed compelled and that it had taken me two hours even though I lived just minutes away.

Miriam was way ahead of me on matters of synchronicity of events. She wrote down her name and phone number and said she had some material I might find interesting. I tucked the small piece of paper with her name and number in my wallet. Oddly enough, I put it right behind the sign language alphabet card given to me by the stranger who came to my door that snowy evening nearly fifteen years earlier. Keep in mind that if I had arrived at the meeting on time I would have sat down, listened, and then left. Only by arriving late did I select a seat in the back by Miriam, feel it necessary to explain my lateness, and ask questions. (I'll tell you more about Miriam later.)

Less than a year later another book of great importance entered my life. I was working on a military installation in San Antonio and right across the street from the headquarters where I worked there was a small base exchange (BX). I would go there sometimes during lunch to buy little necessities to save me a stop on the way home.

One day I stopped at the BX during my lunch hour just to look around. There was a magazine and book section where I noticed a book with Shirley MacLaine's picture on the front. She has always been one of my favorite actresses so I gave the book a look. I put it back on the shelf and then picked it up again. I assumed it to be a biography and thought it would be interesting to read but my life was far too hectic to have time to read such a book. I decided not to get it and was about to check out when I went back to look at the book again. Once again I decided not to buy it and got back in line to pay for my other purchases. Still undecided, I let the lady behind me check out. Then I walked back to the book again. At that point I started wondering why I had so much trouble making this simple decision of buying a book. It was just a book that I did not have time to read so I declined once more. I returned to the cashier and just as she rang everything up and gave me my total, I quickly asked, "Can you still add something else to this sale? I've decided to buy a book I was looking at." She said, "Sure." I grabbed the book, paid, and left.

Weeks went by and I kept looking at this book on my nightstand. I finally made up my mind to read it even if I could only read a few pages each night before I went to sleep. I would read it a while and lose interest. I would pick it up another time and read some more and lose interest. About halfway through the book I marked my place and put it in a drawer. It was primarily about her love life and I just could not get interested.

Only a few days after abandoning the book, one of the girls at work needed to use some equipment directly behind my desk. She sat there working only inches from me. A few of her friends gathered around at lunchtime to make plans. They were very chatty and it was disturbing my work. I was just about to ask them if they could gather elsewhere when my work associate asked her friends, "Have you read Shirley MacLaine's book *Out on a Limb*?" It stopped me in my tracks and I listened to every word that followed. One of the girls said she had heard of it and asked what it was about. My co-worker explained that it was all about reincarnation and how interesting it was.

That did it! There was that Edgar Cayce reincarnation stuff again. After work I went straight home and opened the book and did not stop until I got to something that sounded like reincarnation to me. It turned out to be a great book and an important preparation for more education to come.

About two years or so after meeting Miriam at the A.R.E. meeting, I called her. She remembered me and I said, "Please, if you have information that can help me make sense out of my life, send it to me." I blurted out that my marriage was ending, that I had quit my government work after twenty-one years, and a myriad of other issues that I had never shared with anyone. She was so comforting and supportive and she talked to me about the importance of meditation. I had no idea what she was talking about. She sent me the most incredible little book on meditation and another little book called *Consciously Creating Circumstances* by George Winslow Plummer. I read them over and over. I spoke with Miriam a few more times and shared some of my needs. She encouraged me to get in touch with a lady named Joyce Walker. I had never in my life had a support system, so in my usual way of trying to do everything myself, I put off making that call. Each time I spoke with Miriam she encouraged me to call Joyce, saying that she could help me, but Miriam would never say how.

I finally called Joyce and she invited me to come to her weekly A.R.E. meetings on Monday nights. I began attending and learning about the power of our thoughts and words. I learned how reincarnation and karma work and how we are in control of our life as well as responsible for everything that happens or does not happen. This was a lot for a girl who grew up attending a fundamentalist church and was in the depths of emotional trauma that was "everyone's fault but mine." How the A.R.E. group put up with all my questions and objections, I'll never know. It was a special group of people and they, along with Miriam, taught me how to save my life and my sanity.

One Monday night I arrived early at the group meeting. This was the same night I told Joyce about my visitor and the footprints in the snow. She gave me a small book titled *Treasure Mapping* which is about putting what you want on paper. Through pictures you depict what you want to happen. It becomes a visual affirmation and a statement of faith that it is completed. I made a treasure map on a large poster board and on it I drew the completion of three events that needed to occur in my life immediately. I needed to sell my home, secure employment, and find a temporary place to live. I drew a picture of my home with a sold sign in the yard and the price I wanted. I drew a picture of me sitting at a desk and the salary I wanted. I drew a picture of me sleeping very peacefully in a bed in a nice room. As prescribed in the book I wrote a big "thank you" across the top, then set it aside and "considered it done."

I continued to prepare to move. If I found myself starting to worry, I took a deep breath and said, "It's on the treasure map. I consider it done. Handle it, God, I have packing to do." Within three days the treasure map and the faith behind it had worked its miracles.

I received a call from an employment agency asking me if I was still available. I told her I was and her next question was, "Can you start work tomorrow?" This was a job for which I had interviewed two months earlier. After interviewing me, they decided not to "fire" the person currently in the position. In the meantime she had once again performed in a detrimental way and the CEO put out the call to hire me if still possible.

I also received a phone call in response to my ad to sell the house. They loved it and had just enough money to complete the transaction. They had been looking a long time for a home. They could afford payments, but they had no down payment. I was offering a loan assumption and I had no equity in the home so it worked perfectly for both of us. This was the only call I received on the house ad.

The house sold on Sunday and I couldn't wait for the Monday A.R.E. meeting to tell Joyce how my treasure map had worked so quickly on two of my items. She was not surprised, but when I said there was just one more item to be completed, she asked, "What is it?" I told her that I really needed a place to stay until I had worked long enough to save some money and find an apartment. She then told me that her aging mother loved to have people stay with her and she would arrange for us to meet. Her mother, Rhoda, became a dear friend. I lived with her for several months and I got much more out of it than a place to stay. This is what Miriam had meant when she said Joyce could help me. She knew there was a possibility for me to stay with Rhoda, but all this time Joyce appropriately waited for me to mention it first. When everyone's intentions are working toward good, everything works out in perfect timing. This fact must be trusted. My time in that study group was more valuable than any material treasures this world can offer.

A short time later I shared with Joyce my near-death experience mentioned at the beginning of this book. I explained to her that I had not shared this experience with anyone in the past eighteen years. It had not occurred to me that our wonderful English language would be so limited when trying to describe such an event. When I finished the story there was no surprise or disbelief. What I got was a smile and a casual comment saying that this was not an uncommon experience. I listened in amazement as she told me of Dr. Raymond Moody's book called *Life After Life*.

I began a search for *Life After Life* but was told it was out of print. I called and visited bookstores and I asked all of my new-found metaphysical friends if they had a copy of it. I could not stop looking for the book. I had called every bookstore in San Antonio, Texas, and in a couple of surrounding towns. One Saturday morning I woke up with an incredible sense of purpose and heard myself say, "I'm going to find that book." I headed directly to a large new bookstore a few miles away. I had already phoned that store twice and both times I was told they did not have it and could not get it. I was not sure what I thought I could accomplish in person, but I had to keep looking. I needed to read that book.

I arrived at the Book Stop, parked my car, and started walking toward the store with great deliberateness. The building was built on a slight hill so I had to take steps at the end of a long, elevated walkway that ran along the front of the store. Up the steps and down the walk I went. In my rush I entered the first door I came to. I was standing in a small, dark, slightly disheveled used bookstore. I thought perhaps it was an annex to the big new bookstore. This surprise created merely a slight hesitation on my part. I walked straight ahead, between rows of books to the back of the store, turned right, and went up the last row of books and followed it to the end where I stopped and just stood facing books on the shelf. The shelves were not marked in any way but as I started reading book titles, it was apparent I had walked directly to the metaphysical section. The store clerk caught up with me and asked if there was anything she could help me with. "I seem to have walked straight to your metaphysical section," I replied. "Are they in any particular order?" She said they were not and that there were many more in the boxes directly behind me if I wanted to go through them.

I do not know how I knew, but I knew that book was behind me. So many incredible things had begun happening since I began meditating, using affirmations, and keeping karma in mind with every word I spoke. I was shaking, afraid to turn around. It would not have surprised me to hear the theme song from *The Twilight Zone* start flowing out of the store's stereo system. I slowly turned around.

I was now looking at several boxes of books, but directly in front of me was a box that had been stacked on top of another. The books inside it were within reach. There was one book that was slightly wedged in between the other books just by its corner. It was sticking up and out of the box as if it were reaching up to shake hands with me. My sight was perfectly lined up with the angle of the book so I could not see its front or back, just the edges of the pages. I remember my hands were shaking as I reached for the book. I plucked it carefully from its precarious position, turned it over, and read, *Life After Life* by Dr. Raymond Moody. I found it impossible to move. I stood there and read the title a few more times before the experience started feeling real. I made the purchase and returned home.

The next time you have an unreasonable urge to go somewhere or do something, go ahead. There may be something wonderful waiting for you.

About this same time, I was concerned about a particular health issue with my daughter. I had been convinced that sugar intake was a serious problem for her. I was giving her herbs but became concerned that I might not be working on the correct problem. I began a daily affirmation to bring the answer to me and prayers of thanks for doing so. In my study group I was learning how to pray, how to think, and how to speak to get what I wanted in life. It was working for me.

The next day I was moving some furniture around. I tried to move a chair that had been my grandfather's. It was so big and heavy I could not get a grip on it without taking out the seat cushion. Under the cushion was a ten-year-old issue of *Reader's Digest* and the title on the front cover in big letters was "I'm Joe's Pancreas." It was an article about how sugar is regulated in the body. That chair had been with me for years and I had moved it many times. Not just around the room, but from home to home. The seat cushion had been out of that chair many times. How did a ten-year-old issue of *Reader's Digest* on the subject of sugar in the body get in Grandpa's chair almost immediately after I asked for guidance in that area?

Books seem to be one of the easiest ways for the Universe to guide us to information we need at the time we need it. Even today I can be wondering about something and within twenty-four hours I will hear an author doing a book review on the radio about the subject. I have had books fall off shelves in bookstores right in front of me. I have found books pertinent to a current situation stuck between books in a totally unrelated section or in the grocery store on a shelf with the canned vegetables.

Recently I was in a bookstore and walked by a clerk who was returning a book to the shelf. As I passed, she asked if there was anything she could help me find. Whatever made me say the following I will never know but I said, "I'm not looking for anything particular and books I'm really supposed to read usually just jump off the shelf at me." At the instant of my last word, a book flew off the top shelf with gusto and landed at my feet.

Trying not to laugh, I looked at the sales clerk. Her eyes were now twice their previous size and she looked as if she had been hit with a stun gun. She raised her arms straight up in the air, turned, and walked away shaking her head.

One of the more influential books to come to me was *The Game of Life and How to Play It* by Florence Scovel Shinn. A neighbor dropped by, one I knew only in passing, and she asked me if I had ever read it. I said no, so she returned to her home and brought it to me. It is a book I have read countless times. This little book is strictly about the power of our thoughts and words and how they create circumstances in our lives. I had learned these principles in my group and used them effectively but *The Game of Life and How to Play It* helped embed them in my consciousness making it easier for me to practice.

For many years I purchased this book in quantities of ten and gave them to people who came to me searching for answers. Many of them have told me the book changed their lives. I have done the same thing with *Consciously Creating Circumstances*. These two books explain the basic metaphysical principles in an understanding way. They are a *must* for the beginner. I liken reading these two books to learning the alphabet before learning to read. I still read them to keep me centered in the basics.

I believe the following book to be one of the very best metaphysical books ever written—certainly the best of the vast quantity I have read. I came across *The Dynamic Laws of Prosperity* on one of my many visits to my favorite metaphysical bookstore in San Antonio, Texas, The Unlimited Thought Foundation Bookstore. I was living in Dallas at the time but could not resist the opportunity to go to the UTF Bookstore while in town visiting friends. Author Catherine Ponder has written many prosperity books based on metaphysical principles, but every paragraph in *The Dynamic Laws of Prosperity* has something to say. It is powerful. When I find myself too wrapped up in daily earthly issues and need to remind myself about positive thought and faith, I pick up Ms. Ponder's book, open it anywhere and start reading. I have done so for many years.

If you have questions of a spiritual nature or need guidance for a specific situation, expect the answers and believe they will come. Then stay alert. Answers can come by way of a book finding its way to your desk or by overhearing a conversation in a coffee shop. Anything can be an instrument of inspiration. Do not limit the Universe on its means of communication with you. It could come through a book, the television or radio, a piece of paper you find or in the comment of a child.

It is important to keep ourselves reminded of our beliefs and books are an excellent way to do that. Just knowing the principles of Universal Law is not enough. They must be practiced and lived until they are as natural as walking or breathing.

Chapter Ten
Psychic Readings

Psychic readers have helped many people over the years including myself. I must say that my first experience with a "reading" of any sort was with a charming lady in the hills of Tennessee who read coffee grounds.

My father has two younger twin sisters, Pat and Betty, whom I love dearly. When I was twelve years old the twins took my sister and me on a trip to visit their friends in Tennessee. Pat was engaged and Betty was married with a three-year-old daughter. In the summer of 1959 we loaded up Aunt Pat's small foreign compact car with clothing and bedding for the five of us, along with musical instruments and an amplifier and headed to the hills.

We stayed at the home of a delightful lady whom we all called "Grandma." She seemed content with her life on this Tennessee hilltop with relatives and friends sprinkled around on lower levels of the green, lush mound. Grandma read coffee grounds. I had never heard of such a thing and I was more interested in sitting on the porch, singing country music, and playing with my little cousin. Everyone's reading turned out quite interesting, so I finally agreed to drink a small amount of coffee and let Grandma read my grounds. Over the next couple of decades her words often rang clearly in my memory along with the compassionate, almost frightened look she gave me. She looked at my cup, started to say something, and stopped. She looked again and started to say something and stopped. On her third try she gave her head a slight shake and said, "My girl, you are far too young to hear all this." She turned the cup upside down and my reading was over.

Even though I believe she did the right thing in not telling me, I still wonder on occasion what she saw. As I look back at things (which were still ahead of me at that time), I realize that I might have been psychologically paralyzed and socially crippled had I heard them. On the other hand, perhaps I could have prevented some. Possibly, through understanding, love and meeting responsibilities I did circumvent unpleasantries. The road not traveled is an eternal mystery.

As an adult, the first psychic/tarot reader I visited was referred to as a fortuneteller. I lived in Ohio but she was just across the Indiana border and of course people saw her in great secrecy. Although it had been some time since anyone was burned at the stake for such activities, most psychic practitioners were still thought of as fakes or evil. She was neither. I was nineteen years old, a single parent, but once or twice a year I was able to spend the five dollars she charged to hear words of encouragement. I was not getting them anywhere else. Without fail she would always tell me that I would travel beyond my wildest dreams. I certainly did dream of beautiful far away places, but trying to be sure I ate at least once a day took priority over a travel fund. She seemed so sure and she told me every time. Her words became my dream and that dream sustained me. Roughly ten years later I accepted a job assignment in Europe and indeed traveled beyond my wildest dreams.

After years of receiving psychic advice and later working as a psychic advisor myself, I have made many observations and formed many opinions on this subject. I offer some of it here for you to consider.

Unfortunately there are many *fake* readers who just want to take as much money from you as possible. If someone asks for large sums of money just to say prayers for you or do magic spells or break a curse, grab your wallet and run like hell. But I will only be addressing legitimate, credible, and spiritually minded readers.

I want to present various aspects of receiving a psychic reading. I will not try to talk you into it or out of it. There are pros and cons and it varies from person to person and situation to situation. I just want you to understand the process so you can use it or not use it in the best way possible.

Psychic advice is only as good as it is interpreted, and that isn't easy. Even the best of readers can misinterpret information or have timing of events be off. A psychic friend of mine once told me that my daughter would be moving to California in February. This disturbed me, but February came and went and no move to California. However, she later entered the Navy, went away to training and eventually, in February, moved to California for her first assignment. The prediction was accurate but the timing was off by two years. I assure you, information can come in some cryptic formats.

The biggest problem with using presumed knowledge about your future is that it is nearly impossible not to alter events once you have that information. Let me give you an example.

An acquaintance of mine in Texas visited the psychic mentioned above and shared her experience with me. This lady was in her late twenties or early thirties and had not had many boyfriends, but she recently had a few dates with a very nice young man and they were both excited about all the fun they were having together. She was thrilled when her reading indicated that her new boyfriend would ask her to marry after only dating about six months. She was so excited that on her next date she told him that a psychic said he was going to propose soon and they would be married very quickly. This young man, who had been very excited about this relationship, bolted and ran. He was never given the opportunity to grow into that strong love and marriage that was predicted. The last I knew, she was still single.

It is extremely important to remember that what is predicted is based entirely on what would happen if everything were to happen exactly as it would have if you had *not* had the prediction. This is very difficult.

A receptionist who worked for me wanted to have a reading. She was either divorced or widowed and the mother of an eight-year-old boy. I referred her to the same psychic who happened to live only a few blocks from where we worked. She went on her lunch hour and was quite excited when she returned. She told me that she was supposed to meet a man named George and he would be good for both her and her son. I had cautioned her ahead of time that what was seen may happen tomorrow or a few years from now and that she would have to be careful not to alter any of her behavior after the reading. Although she seemed to understand this prior to the reading, she was now looking around every corner for George. Within a week she could not understand why she had not met him. One Monday morning not long after the reading I greeted her and asked how her weekend went. She said it was fine but she had not done much. She had been asked out to a party but declined because his name was not George.

At that moment I deeply regretted referring this nice lady for a reading. My comments to her went something like this. "What if you were to meet George at the party? What if his real name was George but he went by his middle name? What if he had a good friend named George you would meet later? If you are waiting for George to walk up and ring your doorbell, you'll probably be waiting a while."

These were true events, but let me present some hypothetical situations for you.

People often seek advice on getting jobs. Say your reader told you that you would find a wonderful position in mid to late August. If it is only June, you may quit looking so hard until late

July or so. What if fulfilling the prediction involved an application that you would have otherwise mailed in early July that resulted in your new career? You would have missed it and just thought the psychic was incorrect. More importantly, you would have missed a career opportunity. In this case, the information about August should have allowed you to be less stressed in the unfruitful weeks ahead and given you faith that all would be well. But the information should not have altered any effort you would have normally put forth.

Remember, the power to create your future is within you. A reading can have benefits if used correctly, but the power is within you. The reader is no more powerful than you are.

The example of my acquaintance telling her boyfriend that he would propose, although true, is certainly extreme and most people would be wise enough not to make that specific mistake. A response similar to that given below might be more typical.

What if the reader says your boyfriend will propose so you wait and wait. Since you believe the proposal is coming, you see no need to initiate any conversations on the subject or let him know what kind of future you want. Perhaps you would have otherwise reached a point in the relationship where you told him it was time to move the relationship forward or move on. (Some people need to hear that.) But because of the reading you did not, and the relationship faded away in disappointment. Every relationship reaches a point where the timing is right for such a change. If it is missed, it often never comes again.

Another problem can arise when you know a really good psychic and his or her advice has helped you repeatedly. It is easy to become dependent and trust that person's opinion more than your own instincts. The ultimate goal for all of us is to live a successful life using our own finely tuned intuition and insight.

Psychics have their gift for a reason. They are here to serve. I only caution you on *how to use* the advice given. When I was giving readings regularly, I started each day with a prayer to always be of service, to do no harm, and to guide people in a way that they would improve their circumstances and not alter anything good that is already on their path. I believe I was able to do that in most cases. Below I share two of my readings that point out how a reading can help.

The Rose

A reader needs to be especially concerned when consulting with someone who is in emotional stress or pain. I remember a phone reading for a lady, Mary, who lived back in the Midwest. She was about forty-five to fifty years old and her mother had passed away about a year earlier. They were extremely close and she was still grieving her. They did everything together in years past and in recent years she had cared for her mother around the clock. She had never married nor had a serious relationship. Mary's life was full and she had been happy. There was no need.

Since her mother's death, Mary met a man who wanted to marry her and move her to another state, as his business and property were there. He was financially established, she loved him, and she wanted the life he offered. But she could not bring herself to leave the city of her mother's grave.

Mary knew this was extreme and was looking for someone to give her a way to get past it. Her mother had not been controlling in any way. They genuinely loved each other as mother and daughter and had had great fun together. She believed her mother would want her to take this opportunity but she felt stuck. Intellectually she saw the situation just as most people would, but emotionally she was at a standstill. She had never spoken with a psychic reader before but said she wanted some magic words to help her move on.

Even before she told me about her mother, I let her know there was a very loving female spirit with me and it felt like a mother or possibly grandmother and the connection was very strong. I also used numerology for both her and her boyfriend. It was definitely the right time for her to make this big change. She was finding comfort in everything I said, and when I told her what I felt her mother was trying to convey she said, "I'm sure that is just what she would say to me." However, at this point I was not sure I had told her anything she did not already know.

Toward the end of the reading I began seeing the image of a growing rose. It started with a piece of stem, growing some leaves, more stem, more leaves, and eventually a rosebud that opened slowly into a beautiful red rose. I remember thinking, "How cool is this?" but I kept right on talking. My ideas and choice of words for the client were just perfect and they came to me from this developing rose. Each piece of stem and each leaf as it developed conveyed to me a complete and precise thought to share with her.

In the end, the client was pleased and knew my words were wise. I usually do not share with people how information comes to me, but I was so impressed with this image I received to help me guide her that I said, "These were not just simple words of wisdom or good advice. Let me share with you how these last few minutes came to me. You are being very guided here."

I told Mary about the rose and how clearly it informed me on what to say. She burst into tears, and an apology came flying out of my mouth. "I am so sorry. I guess I underestimated how much pain you are still in and I shouldn't have sounded so excited about the rose. It's not something I would usually do." By now she was crying too hard to talk. I felt just terrible but kept trying to comfort her as much as possible. Soon there was a faint voice. She said, "No, you don't understand. It's not your fault. When Mother was dying she told me she would try to communicate with me from the other side and she would try to do it through a rose." Now she knew this came from *Mom*, not me.

She thanked me for the reading and said she felt completely free to marry and move on to a new life.

That reading blessed me *at least* as much as it did the client.

The Accident

I was reading for a young lady who had been in a very serious automobile accident. Jane's life had been standing still since the accident and she did not know why. Perhaps she was stuck in the trauma of nearly dying, or too afraid to be active in life for fear it might happen again. She just wanted help.

As the reading began I sensed a trauma but I was only aware of a very loud noise. Then she told me she had been in a car accident, saying nothing of its severity. Instantly I had an image and told her, "Your father saved you." She replied that her father was dead and I said, "I know. But he saved you. What I am seeing is your father reaching in through the front window over the steering wheel and pulling you out. Then he sort of flies away with you just as the impact happens."

After a few quiet moments, she told me that she had in fact flown through the windshield of the car and that had saved her life. Normally being ejected is the kiss of death, but she had gone through the window and landed safely with minimal injuries. Then, in a whisper, she said, "I heard his voice just an instant before the impact."

My only comment was, "Well, he did it so you could live. Not so you could be stuck." I heard her take a long, slow, deep breath. I could almost hear her taking in fresh oxygen and letting out fear and anxiety.

What exactly about this reading made a difference? I'm not sure. Maybe she just needed some understanding about hearing her deceased father's voice. Her entire manner of conversing changed after that deep breath and I believe she was ready to move forward.

One of the ways psychic advice can be especially useful is to help you interpret signs or understand experiences you may be having. My situation with the night people is a good example. Here's another.

Not long after moving to Dallas, I had a persistent spirit visit me by way of fragrance. This was not a new thing for me. I've had a wonderful fragrance come to me ever since I was a child. I was in my late thirties before I realized that fragrances can be spirits, but nonetheless it was a familiar experience and did not disturb me. At this point in my life I was so spiritually centered that I found it quite comforting. It was like confirmation that I was living in harmony with another dimension.

This was, however, a different scent from the one that came to me in my early years. Back then I used to sniff around like a little puppy to find out what smelled so good. The fragrance would be only in a small area and right in the middle of nowhere. Try as I might, I never figured out what smelled so good. Something about the aroma always reminded me of childhood Christmases. Perhaps it first began coming to me around Christmas.

This new fragrance was just as unique and it was there constantly. It would follow me around. It would be near me on the couch and if I moved to another room for more than a few minutes, it came to me there. The aroma was contained in a small area about the size of a basketball that just hung in the air.

After a few weeks of this, I developed a sense of urgency about this spirit. I felt it must have a message for me. I talked to it, meditated on it, and prayed about it, but did not get the message. This went on for several weeks so I finally called a more psychically astute friend. I told Beth about the entity and how it followed me around as if trying to get my attention.

Beth immediately asked if it smelled like violets. I said, "No. It is not a fragrance I can describe. It is not like any other smell. It is not like flowers or fruit, nor is it exactly sweet. It is wonderful, but not describable."

All through our conversation she kept telling me she sees violets and felt sure this had something to do with my mother or an aunt. She felt there really was not much more she could tell me unless we could figure out what the violets meant because the image of violets would not leave her.

Bingo! All at once I remembered something I'd heard when I was quite young. My mother had a little sister who died when she was about four or five years old. That makes her an aunt on my mother's side and her name was Violet. My mother had been quite a bit older and took care of this little sister. After getting past that, my friend was able to tell me the message was simply that Violet was always with my mother and watching over her. I told my mother this and the fragrance quit coming. My father then told me that he smells a nice but unusual fragrance around the house from time to time.

In summary, it is important to understand that life is made up of our choices. When a psychic, even a very accurate one, tells you something that will happen in the future, it can cause you to make different choices. It is like a boat headed into shore. Depending on its specific course at a given moment, you can calculate (predict) exactly where it will hit shore. The most minute change in course can alter that landing site by miles.

Let's say you want to change an outcome. Keeping the boat example in mind, if you are close to shore (things not far in the future), you may have to make a dramatic change in your course to hit the shore in a noticeably different location. If the boat were far from shore (things farther out in the future), it would take the most minute change to seriously alter your destination.

It is so important to understand the power of our thoughts, words, and deeds to navigate our boats correctly while still far from shore. Our decisions and our every action are what will keep us from hitting other boats, landing in an undesirable location, or being lost at sea.

If you feel you need advice, seek it. Use it wisely. Many difficult situations have been corrected or avoided by such advice. But keep in mind that you alone are responsible for your actions and what they create. Not your advisor.

Perhaps the most important message for any of us from the gifted mediums/psychics who dedicate their talent and energy to helping others is that there are other dimensions and sources of information beyond our eyes and ears and that we do not die when we leave this body. That alone can change a person's consciousness enough to change his or her whole life.

Chapter Eleven
The Power of Thoughts and Words

One of the best things to happen to me was in 1986 when I began attending the A.R.E. (Association for Research and Enlightenment) study group. In many cases, my own personal experiences confirmed what I was hearing in our meetings and in other cases these new concepts confirmed my experiences. Either way, I had new rules to follow that made sense and gave me power and understanding over all circumstances in my life. In addition, all the members of the group attended Unity Church and I followed suit. The combination of the Unity Church of San Antonio and Joyce Walker's A.R.E. group was magic.

Could it really be that simple? Think it and have it? Think it and do it? Stop thinking it and it will go away? Aside from a few obviously poor choices on my part, I did not feel responsible for the many difficult events in my life. To accept these new concepts I would have to take complete responsibility for everything that has ever happened in my life—even those events and circumstances which previously, and by almost anyone's standards, were *someone else's fault*. Could I do that?

I jumped in with both feet and became a walking, talking, living, breathing affirmation machine. It became impossible for me to have a negative or limited thought. It was working. It was almost scary.

Bless my little study group. They put up with nothing less than a bombardment of questions and instant arguments against their answers. They successfully met the challenge of this new group member. It was not long before karma and reincarnation made as much sense as breathing. Everything I had doubted was clarified. God made sense. Existence made sense. Difficult relationships made sense. I had accepted complete responsibility for everything in my life and all previous lives. More importantly, I took responsibility for creating my future. Although new and enlightening, these teachings triggered a familiarity with that infinite knowledge which had been shared with me so long ago, alone in a hospital room when I chose to remain earthbound.

There are some basic principles which need to be not just understood but brought so completely into your consciousness that it is as natural as opening your eyes in the morning.

Thoughts are energy*:* Thought waves can be measured with the proper instruments. We also know energy does not just disappear. Thoughts go forth, slow down, and manifest into form. It is vital to control your thoughts. If you are thinking that there are no good jobs out there or that everything always goes wrong or that you never win anything, that is exactly what you are creating. When I lived in Europe, I knew a woman who played bingo three nights a week. She always won pretty large sums of money. She looked forward to playing and she made her announcements every morning after bingo about her winnings. I asked her once if she ever played and did not win. I will never forget the look on her face. Her look seemed to say, "Why would I do that?" But her words said, "I don't play to lose, I play to win." She continued to look puzzled, and walked away.

This co-worker could do everything wrong and everything would turn out fine. Why? She expected it to. She was incredibly charming and delightful, though not widely experienced or very curious. All her mind cared to think about was the result she wanted. *Now* seemed to be her whole reality. She is a perfect example of how your thoughts and words work very powerfully even if you do not understand these principles. This is why many people become very successful without ever understanding this power or having any spiritual beliefs. They are focused and determined. They are positive and move forward with intention. However, understanding how your thoughts and words work allows you to put more faith behind them, giving them even more power. It also keeps you from creating negative situations in other areas of your life. Think about how many people have great careers (because of focus and determination), yet have very complicated or unhappy personal lives.

Every time you change your thoughts you change your future. Every time you learn something new you change your future. Every bit of information you learn is more information you have to bring into every decision-making process and that will always impact the outcome. These may seem like minor adjustments at the time, but remember that if a boat traveling across a lake were to change its course by only one degree, it would end up many miles from its original destination by the time it got to shore. The farther it is from its destination when the change is made, the bigger the difference in where the boat lands—so it is with life. When you are young (farther from shore) the small adjustments make bigger differences in where your life ends up. As adults we need to fill the minds of our children with good positive thoughts so they can create a good positive life and land as close as possible to their desired destination.

Intention: Intention works like a silent, positive affirmation to help propel you to your goal. Everything you think, speak, feel, do, or intend is creating your life's experiences. If you do an act of kindness or generosity and your intention is to get your name in the paper to promote your business, you have actually performed an act of selfishness. If your intention is truly to help someone and your heart is filled with kindness and generosity, you will indeed reap whatever benefits are appropriate. If your intention was a selfish motivation, the attention could just open your business to public scrutiny. The intention behind any action will flavor the action accordingly.

You may be recalling that you see people doing greedy, selfish acts all the time and that these people get away with it. Not to worry. They may end up in a very bad business deal ten years down the road and lose everything or perhaps they have greedy employees who are stealing from the company. Keeping score is God's business.

Affirmations: These are positive statements of what you intend to bring about in your life. Always state them in the present tense such as: *I am happy with my work and my pay is excellent.* Say this all the time, believe it, KNOW it will happen, and then pay close attention to opportunities that come your way. When we use affirmations and faith to bring desired circumstances into our lives, they can appear from totally different directions than we might look for ourselves. Remember *mysterious ways*. Be mindful of your intention and faith. Do not use an affirmation and then think to yourself, "I'll try it and see if it works." Guard closely your attitude and faith. They are the fuel for your affirmation. When speaking positive statements like, "I believe I can get a better job," don't follow it with, "but the economy is so poor right now." You have totally neutralized your previous positive statement.

Everything is good: The very first thing you must do in a difficult circumstance is to declare it good. I used this one a lot when I first practiced these spiritual concepts and encountered a difficult situation. I would declare, "Good will come from this," and it always did. Say it with intention and faith. KNOW it is so. Initially I was not very quick at coming up with good affirmative statements to correctly fit a situation, so I would just default to the fact that the outcome would be good. Later I could more specifically express my desired outcome. But "good" is "good."

Sometimes the Universe will come up with a better "good" than we can think of on our own—especially during difficult times.

Reincarnation: It is very difficult for me to think there was a time when I did not accept reincarnation. Perhaps intuitively I always did and that is why my religious teachings left me with more questions than answers. We live many lifetimes and have had many different experiences with all the people in our lives. Between lifetimes we review our experiences, plan our next life, and choose our experiences as well as the people with whom we will share those experiences. Keep in mind that every large or small action in our life *will* create a reaction—somewhere, sometime. Past lives have determined many of our experiences and lessons of this life and behavior in this life will create new experiences and lessons to be learned later in this life or even later in another.

"Good Will Come From This"

As mentioned, one of my favorite affirmations is "Good will come from this." When a difficult situation comes up and you cannot possibly see the good in it, this one works. Perhaps the incident was designed by the Universe and will naturally result in a great thing. Perhaps it was a problem that arose from a negative attitude. You cannot know for sure. But you can trust the Universe to make good come from anything. Remember when I was evicted from my apartment? On the surface it was an unjust turn of events that could not have happened at a worse time. In the end, it took my wonderful current situation and perfected it. Even the Bible assures us that all things work toward good for those who believe. Here is one of my favorite "Good will come from this" stories:

In her early twenties, my daughter decided to enlist in military service. So after several visits with the recruiters and a six-month wait for her slot to come open, we had a 5:00 AM appointment to send her off to basic training in the U.S. Navy.

It was an exciting yet tearful morning. Her last minute jitters made her want to find a way out of this and *Mom's* last minute jitters wanted to help her do just that. But I had worked on military installations for over twenty years and career military personnel had been our friends and second family. Although her immediate future appeared a little daunting to her, the lifestyle was not totally foreign.

After a certain period of training time she was allowed phone calls home. Her opening comments for these calls progressed as follows: "You have to get me out of here!" "I'm a squad leader!" "When will you get here for graduation?" Initially she had told me that this training thing was not survivable unless you were in the top ten percent of your class. My response was, "So, be in the top ten percent." At that particular moment she could not consider that feasible so I added, "Sure you can. Just decide, then do it."

She *did* graduate in the top ten percent, she got her choice of specialized technical training schools, and did so well that she was one of five or six individuals selected to go before a review board where she was selected for an early promotion. Apparently she *decided* to do it. Intention is powerful.

I was incredibly proud of her. Few things stir me more than a military graduation parade. My parents and my sister met me in Orlando, Florida, to see her graduate. It was a wonderful day of activities. That night when it was time for her to go back to the barracks, I walked her to the gate to say good night. She thanked me for some of the steps I took in raising her and expressed that she was there in this proud moment of accomplishment because of me. My heart was bursting with pride, love and joy when I told her, "No, Honey. I didn't take on the responsibility in moments when you didn't do so well and I won't take the credit for what you've accomplished. You did *this* all by yourself."

Ultimately it does not matter what anyone does to you or does for you. What matters is what you do with those experiences. It comes down to your choices. She chose well.

A few months later she had finished her technical school and spent some time at home before going off to her first assignment. We made the drive from San Antonio, Texas, to San Jose, California, in her car, which had the appearance of being a much better car than it really was. However, it made the trip and is now immortalized as the star of this story.

Over a short period of time there were several issues with the car and Lisa began wishing she did not have it to bother with or to pay for. She really had no need for a car on her small Navy base, but was stuck with the car payments and repairs for the time being. I suggested she keep thinking positively and perhaps there would come a time when she or a friend really needed transportation and she would be very glad she had it.

One afternoon I got a phone call from a very exasperated daughter telling me she was on her way back to the base from San Francisco with some friends when someone hit her car. Half serious and half poking fun at my perpetual use of affirmations she blurted, "Okay, now what is it I'm supposed to think or say here?" I could hear her efforts to be rational when she really wanted to scream. She had reached her limit. I reminded her that she had wanted a solution about her car and it would be best to think of this as part of the solution and not a problem.

Apparently they were hit pretty hard, but she assured me no one was hurt. At least the other driver had insurance and she was waiting for the insurance adjuster. I suggested she not worry too much about what outcome she expected, just keep repeating, "Good will come from this," and call me after she spoke with the adjuster.

Over the next hour or two there were several phone calls to confer with me as she negotiated with the adjuster. Each time the settlement sounded better and better and each time she received my encouragement that somehow this would end up a very good thing. I reminded her to keep affirming that good *would* come from this. I do not think she needed my advice as much as she needed someone to "think out loud" with under those energized conditions. With each call she sounded more excited and I summarize the last few calls as follows:

> "Now they are talking about totaling the car." She wondered if that would be good and I said it depended on how much they would pay her. Since she did not need the car, if it were totaled she at least would no longer have repairs or insurance to pay.
>
> The next call was to discuss the exact offer the insurance company made to total the car. It was not enough and it would have left her with too much of a balance on the car loan. I suggested she tell him exactly what she needed, otherwise she would want the car repaired.
>
> She was quite excited on the next call. "Mom, you won't believe this!" They had agreed to total the car and were writing her a check for an amount over her loan balance. This was more than she could have ever sold the car for if it were in perfect condition.
>
> The last phone call was a great one. As Lisa was about to leave, the agent told her it would only cost his company money to dispose of the car, so she might as well keep it and he handed her the keys to her car.

Aside from looking a little dinged up and having one headlight dangling like an eye popped out of its socket, the car could be driven. I would say that good came from this situation, wouldn't you? Just a short time later it suffered a major mechanical failure and she sold it for junk. Were it not for the accident, she would have been stuck with the entire balance of her car loan and no car.

Finding Lost Items

We all misplace keys, glasses, or important papers on occasion. Many have lost wallets or Grandma's favorite broach. We can let the mystical, powerful, invisible forces of nature help us reclaim such lost items through the power of our thoughts and spoken words.

Lost Papers

While living in San Antonio, the company I worked for was in the midst of being purchased by a major retailer. In preparation for a very important meeting on Monday, I took a lot of work home for the weekend. I had just moved and my home was full of boxes. In spite of all the personal work at hand, I prepared for Monday.

Monday came and I was ready to face the busy week. Preparing to leave for work at the refreshing hour of six o'clock, I could not find my business papers. Teams of people had flown in for an early morning meeting — a meeting that could not happen without those missing papers. Obviously they were there somewhere, but *somewhere* was not where they needed to be. I needed twelve copies in the conference room by eight o'clock.

After the obligatory moments of panic and search, I sat down and said, "Lord, be my eyes." I am not sure why I chose those words, but instantly I saw a very clear picture in my mind's eye. It was of a stack of boxes and I could see that the papers I needed were between two boxes in the middle of this stack. Here is the real "kicker." I recognized the boxes. It was the stack of five or six boxes in the middle of my bedroom floor. I went there and removed the boxes one at a time until I came to my paperwork. I had no recollection of moving those boxes over the weekend and would never have looked there.

Lost Purse

When I moved from Dallas to Phoenix, my daughter (already living in Phoenix at the time) flew in to help on moving day and share the road trip west. In the afternoon of our second day, the final stretch of the trip, we stopped at a fried chicken restaurant, ate, and hit the road. An hour or so later, Lisa wanted something out of her purse and it was not in the car. In a moment we realized it had been left in the restaurant. Fatigue, excitement, and determination to be in Phoenix by ten o'clock that evening had distracted us.

My daughter's first thoughts were of her new $300 purse and the signed check inside which she had planned to deposit before catching the plane to Dallas. I told her to just keep visualizing herself smiling as her purse was returned to her home in Phoenix. Just see it coming back and feeling good about it.

Neither of us could remember the name of the restaurant but that did not stop us. Lisa drove and visualized and I looked on a map to find the approximate intersection where we had stopped. It was about then that we decided to pull over and stop. Looking at maps, writing things down, and using the cell phone started adding up to a safety issue. And what could anyone use more at a moment like that than the highway patrol pulling up behind you with his lights flashing? We explained the situation and how we thought it was safer to just pull over. The officer was friendly and supportive. He even stayed there for a while with his lights flashing for our safety.

I dialed the information operator on my cell phone and asked her to please hear me out and try to help us. She was wonderful. She read off countless restaurants in the area we described. To do that she had to review addresses and intersection references in their listings. What were the odds that we would get an information operator who was that cooperative? We ultimately came up with a chicken restaurant in the approximate area. We were excited. How many could there be?

We made the call but it was not the right place. Again, we had someone on the other end of the phone willing to help. She asked other employees if they knew the place we might be talking about. We described it by everything we could possibly remember. I believe it was finally a customer who knew the exact place. When they told us the name, we knew it was correct.

I called the number, reached a nice young man who said he had the purse. It had just been turned in. I let Lisa talk with him as he searched the purse and confirmed that everything was there. He was pleased to help and shipped the purse for express delivery. Soon she was smiling as her purse was returned at her front door.

Missing Wallet

Similarly, ten years later my friend Mary Ann called me to say she could not find her wallet. It was hard for her to believe she lost it as she just had it at the grocery store. I advised her to *see* the wallet returning. I said, "See it walking right up to your front door on two legs if necessary—just see it and believe it."

A few days later she called to say that she had answered an unexpected ring of the doorbell and there stood a man with her wallet. He was the owner of a local tavern and he found it in the alley by his trashcans. The money was gone but everything else was there. Her wallet had returned to her front door on two legs.

"My Hand Is Whole and Healthy"

Without a doubt the most faith-demanding situation I have encountered involved a burned hand. There was a pan of hot bacon grease on my stove and as I moved it, some spatters of grease hit the burner, flashed into flame, and spread back into the skillet. I made a quick move toward the sink and the grease poured all over my hand. Now I was standing there with a pan full of fire as well as dozens little flames all over the stove and floor from spilled grease. I knew the little spots of fire would burn out but I had to put the skillet full of fire somewhere because my hand was also on fire. It was covered with flaming grease but I had to move slowly enough to be careful with the skillet. I carefully sat the skillet on another part of the stove then ran cold water on my hand.

About 80 to 90 percent of the back of my hand and fingers looked like cooked chicken meat. The pain was indescribable. I worked in a hospital so my natural reaction was to call and get an address for the hospital's urgent care clinic closest to me. After speaking with the hospital emergency personnel it was clear I needed to be treated.

I drove to the clinic with my right hand resting on the passenger seat in a pan full of ice water. I could not tolerate the burning when it was out of the water but after about ten seconds, the ice water was equally unbearable. So in and out of the water it went until I arrived at the clinic. I entered with my hand in the pan of ice water and it caused a few chuckles until they saw my hand.

After one look the doctor told me I needed to get straight to the hospital and check in. After much resistance from me, she got out a medical book and read to me that if a grease burn is the size of a nickel, hospitalization was necessary because the patient was at extreme risk of infection. Most of my hand was cooked to the bone and my middle finger was so bad it was difficult for me to look at it. The clinic doctor was obviously alarmed. She insisted I go to the hospital and she would make all the arrangements while I was on my way. I might have done that except for one of her earlier comments: "Lois, they will almost certainly amputate at least this finger and do skin grafts over this area."

I vividly remember looking at my hand between dips in the ice water, trying to picture it without that middle finger. Scars from skin grafting didn't concern me but the missing finger did. Was it vanity or functionality? I don't know. But I had gotten myself through many situations with affirmation and prayer and that is the route I chose. I asked the doctor to treat it the best she could. I was counting on a quick injection to relieve the absolutely mind-bending pain, but I had no one to drive me home so she could only write a prescription.

The next thirty minutes might have been the longest of my life. She salved and wrapped my hand slowly and carefully. It was the size of a boxing glove when finished and it took forever. The hand could no longer benefit from ice water and I was allowed no pain medication because I was driving. Then came the inevitable paperwork. I finally said, "Give me my prescription. I'm leaving. You will have to do your paperwork without me."

Eventually, with prescription clinched between my teeth, I drove one-handed to the drugstore across the street. The hand felt as if it were still on fire and had been that way since I was separated from my ice water. It was about midnight when I went crashing through the door of the drugstore waving the prescription in my left hand and calling out for the pharmacist. From across the room I could see he was some distance from his counter and I wanted him front and center by the time I got there. I shouted as I ran toward him, "I need this prescription filled immediately, but first I need two of the pills and a glass of water!" He met me at the pharmacy counter, took the prescription, and quickly delivered the double dose of painkillers and a glass of water. After filling the prescription he asked if there was anything else he could do to help. I questioned the pharmacist as to whether or not it would kill me if I took another pill or two as soon as I got home. He said, "No, but you should at least be sitting down."

On the drive home I was thankful it was the middle of the night so traffic was very moderate. I was driving one-handed, crazy with pain, had two pain pills in me, and tears were flowing so rapidly I could hardly see.

All at once the reality of the situation set in. I gathered my thoughts and started working on a plan to heal my hand. I carefully worked on an affirmation that would be brief and cover all my needs. All the way home I rapidly repeated this affirmation with as much faith as humanly possible: "My hand is whole and healthy. My hand is whole and healthy."

When I arrived at home I paced the floor with pain and repeated my affirmation. I took more pills and decided I needed someone to talk to until the pills started working. I thought if I did not have a distraction I would lose my mind. I called my parents and asked them to just keep talking about anything. They did and I am forever grateful. After the medication began dulling the pain,

I told them goodnight, got comfortable in a big soft chair, and continued my affirmation until I fell asleep.

As promised, I returned to the clinic the next morning, which was Sunday. The doctor's eyes got big when she saw me and tended to me right away. Her first comment was, "I didn't expect you here today. I believed you would be in the hospital or dead. I was just about to call the hospital to see if you checked in."

She unwrapped the hand and could not believe her eyes. Although it was pretty nasty looking there was no sign of infection. She called everyone over to look at it. She said, "This is a miracle. I have never heard of a burn like this not getting worse before it got better." She also told me that if I had gone to the hospital they would have insisted on removing at least one finger. She cleaned, salved, and rewrapped it and asked me to promise her that I would let one of the ER doctors look at it when I got to work the next morning. I did and he was also amazed. It happened that he had specialized in burns at his previous assignment and he meticulously treated my hand with great expertise. He had not had a good burn to work on in a long time and took great care. The doctor could not believe the burn was less than forty-eight hours old. He also did something called debridement, the process of removing debris from the surface of the wound where tissue is dying and scabs are trying to form. It literally involves scrubbing the raw burned tissue. That almost brought me to my knees but I welcomed anything that would support my healing.

I called a friend whom I knew as an astrologer, though she was also a nurse. I needed to cancel a lunch with her and when I told her what had happened she said that she had been a nurse in a burn unit and she would be happy to continue the cleansing of the wound for me. She said it was much too painful for anyone to do on one's own. I continued my affirmation of, "My hand is whole and healthy," and also gave a great deal of thanks for the progress so far and for all the support I was getting. Although it was tender for a long time, I have full use of my hand and there are no scars.

I do not recommend that anyone turn down medical advice or treatment, especially where burns are concerned. I believe it was just my time to exercise my faith in regard to healing and see the results demonstrated. Healing energy has become a very important part of my life.

I say *The Lord's Prayer* many times a day, thinking about every line as I say it. It is one positive affirmation after another. My mind just automatically goes to that prayer when it is not crammed full of other thoughts. It just sits there ready to play as soon as other thoughts go on pause. It is powerful.

Create your own affirmations for specific situations as well as for general circumstances. Do it carefully. Make sure it is complete. When my hand was burned I did not affirm just to save my fingers. If I had they may have healed but been deformed. I affirmed that my hand was whole and healthy. Give your affirmations some thought. Use them well. Leave the Universe some room to improve on your expectations.

Many times when affirming for something to come in to my life I will end it with, "This or something better, Lord." If we get too specific we can limit God's handiwork. If you need a job, affirm something like, "Thank you for my great job and great pay." If you affirm for a specific job or one at a specific company you may be blocking yourself from something better. Words are powerful. Use them well in all things.

Chapter Twelve

Things Come to Me

A good friend and work associate in Dallas used to marvel at how things worked out for me when his own life at the time was a series of small catastrophes. He had a great sense of humor and we had a lot of fun discussing the contrast of our lives. I tried to teach him about positive thinking and affirmations and though he did his best, I do not think he was quite ready. When amazing little things happened I would just look at him and say, "Things come to me."

He observed many of my daily demonstrations, but routine or not, they were demonstrations of how wonderfully fun our lives can be when we expect more and live in a deserving manner. If I were to mention that I needed to talk to another co-worker, that person would walk by within moments. One day when a few of us went to lunch I ordered a small pizza. After several minutes of smelling all the wonderful meals being served, I commented that I should have ordered a medium. When my pizza came, it was a medium. They had made a mistake and thought I would not mind.

One night when our "after work" group headed across the street for happy hour, I told my friend that it had been a really challenging day and I did not know if I could *wait* for Paul (our bartender) to draw my beer. When we walked in, Paul said, "Hey, Lois. Saw you coming and I've got your beer over here waiting for you."

The joys of understanding Universal Law and the power of our own creative abilities extends far beyond turning our desires into affirmations and willing them into existence. It is about the everyday surprises, the interesting and marvelous things that manifest which are beyond our imaginations.

Let us compare it to Christmas. Some children are asked every year to make out a list of what they want and on Christmas morning pretty much everything is under the tree. They look it all over and calculate what, if anything, from their list is missing. In another family the children look forward to Christmas without having made a list. Santa knows in general terms what these children need or want and on Christmas morning everything is a wonderful surprise. Without the list, nothing can possibly be missing and the gifts they love the most might not have even been on their list. These are the children who have the best holiday memories—holding Santa and their families dear in their hearts for their entire lives. The same is true for what we expect and get from the Universe.

Obviously, if you are out of work, you are putting in a specific request for a job. If someone is sick, you are putting in a healing request. It is also perfectly fine to want a new car. It just should not be quite like a Christmas list where everything is very specific and you are always noticing what has not yet manifested; that can be discouraging and limiting. What you are wanting might very well *not be the best possible things* for you at this time. Therefore you could slow down the arrival of a much better option.

It is all about faith. The right answer will come. The right job will come. You will experience many wonderful things. What many people fail to recognize is that happiness is not wrapped up in just the big stuff like the top job, the car, the right neighborhood. That is the old "If I had more money, I'd be happy" syndrome. But there is never enough money because you just spend it and the "stuff" can become a burden and an additional expense. Too many "things" can also become an enormous anchor that can keep you from taking advantage of great opportunities—such as that "perfect" job in another town.

True happiness is often found in what does not happen. There are people who never seem to have *troubles* popping up, who just seem lucky, always having something fun and wonderful to talk about. Then there are people who have constant trouble, seemingly through no fault of their own—their wallet has been stolen twice, the engine seizes up on their relatively new car, their plumbing backs up six hours before a big party, if company payroll hits a glitch it will be their paycheck that is delayed, appliances never work quite right for them.

If your mind and behavior are mixed up and disjointed, you are creating a mixed up and disjointed environment. If your emotional state is intense and out of control, all activities around you will reflect that also. Correcting all things starts with correcting your thinking. Correcting your thoughts will change your feelings and behavior. Changing your feelings and behavior will change everything and everyone's response to you. This boosts your confidence and satisfaction that in turn improves your thoughts and the upward spiral continues.

Your everyday thoughts, words, and actions all have reactions. The pattern of these everyday thoughts and words creates what I call your theme. Your theme is a huge powerful force behind all of that daily activity. Your theme is your core belief system, your value system—those concepts that you put your faith in and act as constant, unspoken affirmations. Your theme is what you have thought and believed for so long that it no longer needs to be said to have an outward effect. This is understood by the Universe as "who you are." These core beliefs are inherently reaffirmed and demonstrated in all that you say and do and all that you experience.

If your core beliefs resemble any of the following, you are at a good starting place for working with your spoken words and intentions to improve your life:

> I am worthy of good things.
> I believe I can accomplish what I set my mind and heart to.
> I believe there are unseen forces that offer me guidance and support.
> I live an honest life and integrity is important to me.
> All things work toward good.
> People can count on me for support.
> It is important to treat people with kindness and respect.
> I feel good about how I live my life.
> There is a higher power Who loves me and wants good things for me.

However, if your beliefs are reflected in or similar to the following negative rhetoric, you will have to do some work before getting a positive response from the Universe:

> If it can go wrong, it will go wrong.
> I never have any luck.
> I hate Mondays.
> I'm not smart enough to go to college or get a great job.
> I'll try an affirmation but it probably won't work.
> Nobody likes me.
> My parents made me this way.
> No one ever gives me a chance.
> If there were a God he wouldn't allow . . .

Energy attracts like energy so get positive, no matter how much work it takes. Replace those negative and limited thoughts. Keep in mind that thoughts cannot be stopped—they have to be replaced. Every time you catch yourself in this defeating dialogue (verbal or mental), stop and turn it around. Use replacement statements such as:

Today is Monday—I'm refreshed and ready for a good week. Everyone cooperates with me today.

I always cringed when I heard someone complaining about Monday, or blaming his or her oversights on Monday. Somewhere along the line this bad habit got started and has yet to be stopped. I have always wondered why people believe Mondays are such tough days. They have had all weekend to rest up, have fun, and get things done. It always seemed to me that if any day deserved to be labeled as difficult it should be Friday when you are running out of steam. Even so, I always used Fridays to look back on how much I had accomplished and I felt really good about it. There is simply no advantage to deliberately forming thoughts that make you feel badly about your day. You are defeated before you start.

Faith and a positive outlook help create a life where things go well. For me, being positive always seemed like a smarter way to live. Why would I want to have an attitude that makes me miserable when I can have an attitude that allows me to look forward to whatever comes next? My early adult years were difficult enough without adding any self-inflicted, moment-to-moment misery through bad attitude and low expectations. It would have made everything unbearable for me. Some people like to call this hope, but I just do not like that word. To me hope *implies* doubt, and where's the faith in that? The next time you are tempted to say, "I hope so," replace it with, "I'm counting on that," and see if you don't feel better.

Employment

It is easy to look back and see that the power of thought manifestation, faith, and expectation was working in my life long before I understood it; it was simply my core beliefs—how I lived my life and what I expected in return. Employment has been a critical element in my life just as it is for almost everyone. I now share with you some great employment stories that I consider among my favorite miracles.

As mentioned earlier, I worked for the U.S. government for a long time. During that time I held many positions. Position changes happened for various reasons such as relocation, promotions, and sometimes because I simply needed a change. I expected to get the job in every interview process—I was dedicated and had a superior evaluation record so I expected the interviewer to recognize I was the best choice. I believed this. I observed employees around me and I strived to be more professional and I worked respectfully with everyone. Because of this, it was easy for me to believe I was an excellent choice in each situation. Career was the one area in my life where I always had confidence—I had control over how well I performed. Good performance records and an excellent attitude put me right up there at the top of interviewers' selection lists. A good performance record and an excellent attitude are both good to have but there is always some little thing that causes the interviewer to choose one person over another. That extra thing is among the many things that the Universe manages for you if you are doing your part.

I was selected for one position because I did not carry a purse to the interview. I dislike carrying a purse so much that I just *don't* unless a situation really requires it. As I was leaving, the gentleman who interviewed me said, "Oh, wait a minute." I waited in the hall as he went back into his office. I was a little puzzled, but I waited. He came back out and asked, "Where is your purse?" I responded, "Why?" He said, "I looked all over and I can't find it." I laughed and told him I did not bring one.

As I was leaving he had noticed that I did not have a purse and assumed I left it in his office. He said women did that all the time in interviews, probably because they were nervous. By the time I got home there was a message on my answering machine saying that any woman secure enough to not carry a purse was the one he wanted working for him.

How many men even notice if a woman is carrying a purse? What caused it to impress him? Even if I had understood the power of affirmations at that time, it would never have occurred to me to go into an interview thinking, "Please let this man notice and be impressed with the fact that I don't have a purse." Do your best and let the Universe do the rest.

Another time during my first week on a new job, my supervisor came to me and asked, "Don't you want to know why I selected you?" I said, "Not really, but I'm glad you did." It was obvious that he wanted to tell me and that intrigued me, so I asked him why.

He explained that it was between another girl and me. We were very equally qualified with very comparable experience. He really liked both of us and felt he could work well with either. He said he could find absolutely nothing to break the tie and he had never encountered that dilemma. One applicant always had something in his or her paperwork that tipped the scale.

He explained that he sat down with both sets of paperwork side by side, compared them back and forth, and found nothing. Then he decided to look at a general information form with our basic personal data like name, address, date of birth, and so on. When he read the place of birth and noticed I was from Ohio, he quickly checked the place of birth for the other applicant. She was from California. He looked at me with a matter-of-fact expression and said, "People from Ohio are the hardest working people I have ever met." He turned and went back to his office.

The following series of events involve the most exciting job experiences of my life. The process was filled with mysterious ways and many wonders were performed.

Having tired of the severe Ohio winters, I made several attempts to transfer to Florida or somewhere in Texas along the Gulf. As could be expected, local state residents received priority in the hiring process, but every so often I gave it another try. I prepared a very professional cover letter to accompany my government application form. Then I selected my most preferred base in Florida to receive this renewed effort toward relocation—Tyndall Air Force Base. On my lunch hour I walked over to the Logistics Command building where there was a post office. With great excitement I purchased and addressed an envelope complete with postage. I sealed it and gave the envelope a quick squeeze and thought, "Please, I need to leave Ohio."

I walked across the small work area where employees prepared their packages and pulled the chute open where we dropped our post. With my left hand holding the door open and my right hand reaching in with the envelope, I heard someone say my name. Surprised, I turned around and saw an old friend I had worked with for several years in that building. I walked toward her as she asked how I was doing. At that point I realized the application was still in my hand. I showed her the envelope and explained that I was mailing another application to Tyndall because I really wanted to get out of this weather.

She said, "Oh, I have a great idea. FTD, the organization across the street, is moving to Tyndall. The whole organization is being relocated. Just transfer over there. It will be an easy transfer and the government will pay for your move to Florida." No need to hear that twice. This was miraculous. I felt so fortunate. I walked straight over to the civilian personnel building and handed them the application I had prepared for Tyndall and said I wanted to transfer to FTD (Foreign Technology Division). A few days later a man walked up to my desk where I was currently working and said, "I understand you want to work at FTD." I was completely alone in my office, which was unusual, so he sat down. We had a little chat and he asked me to come work for him.

To hasten this story, two weeks later I was working at FTD. As I recall, it was only days after that when the headlines of the local newspapers read that the relocation of FTD to an out-of-state base had been successfully blocked to prevent job losses in the area. I would have been devastated except I loved this new organization already. During my years there, I had incredibly exciting work experiences, established friendships that have lasted a lifetime, and after a year or so I received a nice promotion. But I was still in Ohio.

After a series of extraordinarily severe Ohio winters, I was exhausted. I worried endlessly about my daughter walking to and from school in freezing winds and snow. One evening when I got home, and once again had to remove the snowdrifts to get back in my driveway, I shouted a rather determined statement, loud enough for the neighbors to hear: "This is my *last* winter in Ohio." And indeed it was.

A very short time later, the Chief of Staff for the organization offered me an assignment in Europe. It took me all of two minutes to make my decision and say yes. The following June I moved to Germany where the winters were much less severe than Ohio and were indescribably beautiful. I traveled extensively and made memories that delight me to this very day. After Europe I went to San Antonio, Texas, which was a place I had always wanted to live.

All this happened to me because I did not remain rigid about how I would get out of Ohio. I was flexible enough to try a new organization rather than a direct move to Florida. I remained positive when plans to move the organization to Florida changed and I maintained a great work ethic. I saw it as a blessing and it blessed me. I believe there are bigger and better things in store for us than we can imagine, and if we cannot imagine it, how can we ask for it? I wanted to leave Ohio, I had always dreamed of how wonderful it would be to travel in Europe, and San Antonio had captivated my imagination since childhood. For many years I worked hard, tried to do the right things in life, and appreciated everything that was good. I forgave people who did not treat me as well as they should have and I always believed in rising above circumstances. I am reminded of the biblical promise, *"I will restore to you the years that the locust hath eaten" (Joel 2:25).*

This is a great example of how our core beliefs work for us.

Those unspoken desires and good works always return to us. How could I have ever worked up an affirmation that would get a great job, with wonderfully competent people who would soon promote me and who would eventually send me to work in Europe where I could travel extensively? Let's not forget that it also allowed me to end up in Texas. Leave the details to God. Several of my desires were lumped into a series of opportunities of which I took advantage. I have observed that many people do not reach their desired levels of happiness and satisfaction simply because they do not open the door when opportunity knocks. I believe all this unfolded for me because of the everyday things I was doing right — even if they seemed thankless at the time. The *high road* is the only way to the *high life*.

These next employment experiences took place after I learned to employ my faith and affirmations. I consciously worked with Universal Law to secure for myself the best possible position.

While in Texas I left government employment and was excited about working in the civilian world, something I had never done. While there, I worked at the headquarters of a national retail chain. (This is the position I secured through *Treasure Mapping,* which I spoke of in Chapter Nine.) As their corporate office manager I worked with every department of the company as well as many outside vendors. It was an exciting time of expansion for the company. However, after four years, I learned the same lesson that many people did in the eighties: quick growth and over-expansion result in reorganizations and cutbacks. Putting a positive spin on it, I was now free to find something even better.

Initially I was not concerned. Most of the exciting work was over, the new management team was not vested in what we had developed, and I was already thinking about leaving. I spent mornings sending out resumes and afternoons at the pool. Why not? I had worked hard all my life. Why should I not use some of this free time to completely relax?

The previous five years I had been studying spiritual principles, meditating regularly, saying daily affirmations, and was being the best self I could be. I believed with all my heart this transition was a good thing and that I would obtain an even better job, and I did. However, I was not prepared for how long it would take or how it would come about.

After several months of unemployment, I put all my belongings in storage and traveled back and forth between San Antonio and Dallas looking for work. I stayed with Lottie, my downstairs neighbor in San Antonio, and with my friend Judy in Dallas. I wanted the flexibility to accept a position quickly and at any location.

Nine months of job hunting began to test all that I had come to believe and practice. I had interviews in which people told me they were very pleased, asked me if I were available immediately, and said personnel would be in touch with me soon, yet I would receive a call saying they had selected another candidate. I had one interview in which I was told, "You are exactly what we are looking for," but again the call came that I had not been selected. Regarding another position, the CEO was allowing a team of three subordinates to select the best applicant. After interviewing me they told me I was the best candidate and that they would start the paperwork right away, but they wanted me to come in the next day to meet the CEO. I agreed, but later that day I received a call at home saying that the CEO said I could not be hired because he and I had the same last name and someone in the company, or a company they did business with, might think he unfairly hired a relative. After a moment of disbelief it seemed almost funny and I found myself saying, "Well, if he has enough integrity to worry that someone *might* think he did something inappropriate in business, then guess what—we probably are related!" I thanked them for their honesty and pressed on.

I prayed a lot during this time. I used very positive affirmations before each job interview and truly tried to keep smiling. It is very important to mention that I always prayed for the "best possible job for me." After job interviews I gave thanks for their great response, but I always ended my prayers and affirmations with, "This or something better, Lord." I believed with all my heart that there was a right place for me, a place that really needed my skills and would reward me for them. In spite of feeling some desperation now and then, I did not want to be stuck in a dead-end job that did not make good use of my experience. I think my affirmations, attitude, and determination caused employers to want to hire me but later when I said my prayers and added, "This or something better, Lord," the energies changed. The Universe knew I could hold out a little longer for the best option.

How did I get the "something better" job? Here's how miracles work:

One evening, after making the drive back up to Dallas from San Antonio, I was visiting a new friend before continuing on to Judy's. We were watching television and it was getting late. I dreaded the thought of getting back in the car to drive from the south side of Dallas to Judy's far northern suburb. However, Judy and her husband were out of town and I promised I would be back that night to take care of their beloved dog. Sometime shortly after ten o'clock, I jumped up and said that I just had to get on the road. I made the drive and I actually found the night air and light traffic to be relaxing.

I arrived at Judy's front door with all my luggage hanging over my shoulders and on my elbows. As I got to the front door I heard the phone ringing. I tried frantically to find their hidden key and get the door open. My bags were falling off my shoulders and I was falling over the ones I had set down. I remember questioning why I was doing this because I really did not have to answer their phone. The door came open and I jumped over the bags. With the door still standing open I ran to the nearest phone. I grabbed it and yelled, "Hello!" There was a short pause and I thought I had missed the call. Then I heard a questioning voice say, "Lois?"

It was my friend, Ralph. He was the telecommunications vendor for the organization I had previously worked for in San Antonio. His home office was in Dallas but he was calling from out of state—Atlanta, I believe. He had been in Dallas earlier that day in a meeting at a hospital where they had discussed a job opening that he thought was perfect for me.

The amazing part is that he did not know I was staying in Dallas. When he arrived at his hotel he started looking through his briefcase to find my number. He could not find my home number (in San Antonio) and he did not have a copy of my resume with him, which listed all my phone numbers. What he did find was a Dallas number I had given him a long time earlier when I was in Dallas visiting Judy. He thought he would give the number a call on the chance they would have a good number where I could be reached. We could not believe the "coincidences." He said that if their answering machine had picked up, he would not have tried again since the hospital was to make a decision on the position the very next day.

The next morning I called the supervisor in charge of the position Ralph told me about. She said she had already made her selection, but I just kept talking about my qualifications, how highly Ralph spoke of her, and anything I could think of to keep the conversation open. Pretty soon she said, "Well, we have not actually notified the candidate, so why don't you come in and see me." I did and I got the job. I loved working in that hospital system. They needed my experience and I received extraordinary salary increases during the four years I was there. It was the perfect place for me and it was worth the wait.

After settling into my own charming Dallas apartment with a beautiful view, I got curious and wanted to evaluate my finances for the period of time that I had been out of work. Between severance pay, a couple of periods of temporary work, unemployment benefits, and what I saved on rent (thanks to my wonderful friends), it came out almost exactly to the salary of my old job, almost as if I had not been unemployed at all. See how brilliantly the Universe works out its plans for you when you cooperate?

Four years later I made the choice to leave the hospital in

Dallas to move to Phoenix where I could be close to my daughter and grandson. I started buying Phoenix newspapers and sending out applications. One Friday night, with all my friends waiting at a restaurant nearby, I stayed late at the office to finish some paperwork. As I was locking the door to leave, I heard my phone ring. It was after-hours on Friday, yet I unlocked the door and answered the phone. It was from Phoenix in response to my resume and they wanted me to come interview right away. I took a couple days off the next week, interviewed, got the job, returned to Dallas, and gave two weeks' notice. Had my core beliefs been negative or self-centered, I would not even have considered answering a phone after-hours and I would not have known what I missed.

Interestingly, the job turned out to be absolutely the worst employment experience of my life, so I quit. But it did get me to Phoenix. My daughter and her family moved to Oregon only a year and a half later. I considered it a Divine intervention to get me to Phoenix where I could be closer to the kids while I looked for something better. Also, after I left that position, it became necessary for me to work full-time with my spiritual consulting and numerology. That also was incredibly positive for me. However, I wanted full-time employment and I missed having a daily work environment and interacting with colleagues.

Again, I began the ritual of applying for almost everything in the Sunday paper. Most of the jobs for which I interviewed were actually not appealing to me. Time went on and on and I kept believing there was a great job out there for me—any day now. Everyone I spoke with said the economy was bad, you had to "know someone" to get a good job in town, the pay scale in Phoenix was much lower than other cities, and so on. I worked hard to shrug off those limiting thoughts.

One Sunday I looked through the paper and found only one or two ads that I would even consider. I was doing fine with the consulting, but I was ready to have an office to go to, colleagues to say good morning to, and a sense of belonging to an organization.

I missed that. I threw the newspaper in the trash and just decided to skip a week on the job search and went about doing the laundry. A few minutes later I turned toward the trash can and said, "No. There just has to be something in all those ads that is right for me." I retrieved the paper, opened it to the classified section and arbitrarily read an ad right in the middle of a page.

At first I wondered how I could have missed it, then I realized I did not have any of the qualifications they required. It was an ad placed by a German corporation that was looking for someone to start up their first U.S. sales and distribution office. The ad asked for international trade and import/export experience. The thought of working for a German company and possibly being able to travel back to a country I loved deeply was just too appealing to ignore.

I sat down and composed a letter in which I explained that I had none of the experience called for in the ad, then proceeded to list the qualifications I felt they needed for someone to organize and launch their business, followed with just how I could fill all those needs.

One month later they came to Phoenix to interview me. Another month later they flew me to Germany to meet and interview with all the key managers at their company. One month after that I was offered the first position in their new U.S. corporation. As their Vice President of Administration and Chief Financial Officer, I loved the variety of my responsibilities and working in an international environment once again.

Everyday Surprises and Solutions Come Your Way

If you are living well and affirming well, the right things, the right answers, and the right decisions will come. The Universe knows your secret desires as well as your specific requests.

Shortly before I made the move to Germany on my government assignment, I was down to some last-minute details such as selling my car. However, before running an ad to sell the car, I wanted to replace the bumper. The car was six years old and in perfect condition except for the bumper. It had a small dimple-like dent and was ever so slightly corroded. One evening, my daughter and I stopped by a friend's apartment. As we were leaving, we saw one of the neighbors and struck up a conversation. As discussions go, we began talking about my move. I mentioned that everything was pretty much ready except for getting a new bumper for my car. He asked what kind of car it was. When I told him it was a 1971 Maverick, an amazed look came over his face. He said, "I have a 1971 Maverick rear bumper standing on end in the corner of my bedroom. It has been there two years. A friend was going to throw it away and I took it thinking surely there was someone who could use it." Once I got past the notion he was only having a little fun with me, I was the one with an amazed look on my face. I asked how much he would sell it for and he said five dollars. My response, "Sold."

Now, when I look back on that experience with my expanded understanding of Divine design and synchronicity, it is clear that the Universe was planning my move at least two years earlier when a nice young man saved a bumper from the scrap heap. The next time someone else's neighbor strikes up a conversation, do not be so quick to rush off and tend to your busy little schedule. There may be something in it for you. Remember, the Master Planner never sleeps. Every moment is tended to. Work with it.

While working in the hospital system in Dallas, I managed the cell phone program for the physicians. Cell phones were still considered a luxury item and were only becoming commonplace in situations where this ease of communication was essential to the job—such as sales personnel or physicians. Working around this technology naturally made me want one, but it would have been totally for fun and convenience, so I resisted. I was saving money to buy a house and I saw my friends every day at work. I have never been one to spend time on the phone just chatting, so I just had no need for one.

I initiated a program through the cell phone vendor for all

hospital employees to have the opportunity to sign up for cell phones at the same excellent rate that I had negotiated for the physicians. The cellular vendors were so overwhelmed with the response and all the money they made that they gifted me with a free cell phone and all services paid for one year. I had undertaken a very time consuming task strictly for the benefit of my colleagues and my efforts were rewarded. Cause and effect — it is always there. Things like this make me wonder how the word karma acquired its common connotation of "punishment." Put out good "causes" and you will have good "effects."

Sometimes we appear to create uncomfortable situations no matter how good we are. I always trust there is a reason for it and keep on going. A good example of this is the week I spent in Ruidoso, New Mexico. I needed a place to hide away and start arranging some of my writing in a book format. I had attended a wedding in Santa Fe where I had developed a serious allergy problem and was looking forward to a quiet week in Ruidoso in the family vacation home of my friend AnnDee. My first night there I was so sick I thought I would die if I fell asleep. About four in the morning I got dressed and decided to drive for help. As I was walking out to my car, I dropped the garage door opener and it broke into several pieces. I would just have to worry about that later. I needed to get medical care.

I was totally unfamiliar with this rustic little town, but I had to do something. Before long I saw the local police station. I went in to ask directions and the police officer on duty was quite reluctant to let me get back in my car. After assuring him I was capable of driving, I found my way to the local hospital. After being diagnosed with a serious sinus infection, I took my prescriptions and parked in the drive-through of the local drug store and slept until it opened.

After a day or two of drugs and sleeping, I began to work on the problem of the garage door opener. The general consensus of everyone I called was that the opener was obsolete. It was over twenty years old and most of the garage door opener's mechanisms would need to be replaced and the remote opener updated. I was still too sick to work on my writing so I kept making phone calls about the opener. I would not give up. I started saying affirmations that I would find a solution— affirmations that there had to be a suitable opener out there and I would find it.

Not knowing the proximity of all the little New Mexico towns in the area, it was hard to tell by the phone numbers if a business I was calling was local or far away. I eventually found a very sympathetic gentleman who seemed to know all about the particular garage door opener I was trying to replace. He even had me turn it over and asked if there were two screw holes or one on the back. This apparently distinguished it from another similar opener. I told him how kind AnnDee's parents had been to allow me the use of their home for a week and how badly I felt because I had caused an expensive problem. I told him I really needed to fix it in the next few days. I said I truly believed there was another one out there somewhere and I just needed help finding it. Finally he said, "I haven't seen one in about twenty years, but let me walk into the back and see if anyone else knows where you might find one."

He was apparently on a cordless phone because he no sooner finished those words when he said, "Oh my goodness! I don't believe this. There is one right here on the counter. Where did this come from? There's nothing else around it. It's just lying here." He did not know where it came from or why it was there. He rambled on in disbelief for a while and then said I could have it for nothing. Great! But he was two hours away and I was too sick to drive. He said he would be happy to mail it two-day express.

I called AnnDee to ask for the address but she explained there was no mail service to the cabin. I found the local post office, set up a general delivery address, then called the garage door company to tell them how to address it. Two days later I made my way back to the post office and indeed it was there. Now all I had to do was take the plastic casing off the new one and get all the parts of the old one inside and working. Shortly after, with all parts assembled, I pointed it toward the garage and squeezed the button. I could not have been more thrilled if I were watching a NASA launch when that door went up!

What a demonstration of the power of affirmations, faith, and intention. I rested a couple more days then headed home. On the drive home, still not feeling very well, I had time to ponder the events of the week. It occurred to me that while I was at the cabin, my intention had been to organize materials I had written into some order or format for a book, and that this event with the garage door opener demonstrated much, but not all, of what I was writing about. I think the Universe was providing me my topic — it was just what I needed to get started. Even though I lay ill on the couch for a week, I accomplished exactly what I intended. That is the art of recognizing the miracle. Do not let *your* miracles go undetected.

I have this general understanding with the Universe that I would like confirmation from time to time that I am on the right track or that I am doing the right thing. Recently I was gathering items to give to the Salvation Army. On top of one of the boxes of collected goods, I dropped a book called *Your Best Life Now* by Joel Osteen. It was a new, hardback, bestseller. I stopped and questioned why I was giving it away. It was a good book and I typically read books a couple of times then loan them to friends. I took it back off the pile.

Later I put the book back with the donation items then subsequently questioned why I was giving the book away. After three or four goes at this, I said, "That's it. There must be a reason I'm compelled to give this book away. Someone must need it more than I."

A week or so later I received a call from a medical imaging center asking me to return. They needed to run one more test on me. While in the waiting room, I was reading a book and the lady across from me asked what I was reading. I smiled and showed her the cover and went back to my book, avoiding conversation.

Then she said, "You should read this. It is the best book I ever read. This book has changed my life."

I found myself sitting there looking at a lady holding up a copy of *Your Best Life Now*. Unable to resist, I asked, "Do you mind if I ask where you got that book." Her reply, "I got it at the Salvation Army. They have great books there. People read them once and give them away." There was a confirmation if ever there was one. But it was about to get even better. Just then the man who had called me to come in for another test walked up to me and apologized for having me drive all the way there, but they did not need that extra image after all. My response was, "Not a problem. Don't worry about it." I knew exactly why I was there and he had just been a facilitator. How good of God to let me know the impact I helped create by following my instincts and tossing a book on a giveaway pile. Never underestimate the ramifications of any and all actions.

I am not much of a party person but I do like to entertain occasionally—as in having everyone I know over for food and drinks. About a year after moving to Dallas, I wanted very much to have such a gathering but I had given away most of my dishes and glasses before moving, as I like to travel light. I am not a fancy person but I do like things to be nice, and I have a few strong likes and dislikes. Among my dislikes are plastic glasses and paper plates—especially at parties.

I knew I could pick up small glass plates for almost nothing, but how would I get thirty or forty wine glasses? Shortly after the party idea took root in my head, I was sitting at home reading a book when a very good friend called. She was doing some cleaning because she had just bought a house and was giving away everything she was not planning to move. As a successful recovering alcoholic, she offered me her entire collection of stemmed wine glasses. I had enough for a party.

She also offered me her entire bath towel set she had just purchased because they were gray and she wanted a different color in her new home. They were brand new and luxurious. It also happened that on my to-do list for the very next day, I had written *shop for new bath linen, in gray.*

There are two cities that had fascinated me for many years. One was Santa Fe and the other, New Orleans. I really wanted to visit these cities but I knew no one there so they just stayed on my list of things I would like to do one day. Then my closest neighbor moved to Santa Fe and I made several wonderful visits. Santa Fe has great charm and character.

About this same time I got a call from a good friend who just wanted to say hello and see how things were going. We talked for a while and I told him about visiting Santa Fe and how I had always wanted to go there. I mentioned that New Orleans was one more city I had a great curiosity about and that I really wanted to see. After a brief pause he said, "I'm leaving for New Orleans in a couple of days. I have a free airline ticket I'll never have time to use, so if you want to tag along and see the city while I'm conducting business you are quite welcome to it." I did. I only had about a day and a half there, but I took a city tour, walked the streets, and ate the food. It was delightful and incredibly interesting.

Answers can come in amazing ways if you listen to your instincts. After the German company I worked for was sold to a large high-tech firm I was once again in a career decision-making process. I felt I really needed a change. Should I look for another job? Should I pursue artistic endeavors with my photographic art, which had been only a hobby? Should I write a book? Should I go to school and train for something entirely different?

Pondering these questions one sleepless night, I was channel-surfing late-night television and one of the church programs caught my attention. This particular minister was easy to listen to, but I often questioned his Bible references. He spit out chapter and verse references faster than most of us can spit out names of family members. His messages were pretty good so I always felt a little guilty about suspecting his accuracy. After a long string of Biblical quotes, I jumped up and said, "I'm checking that last one out." Even though I can quote many passages, I am not the least bit proficient when it comes to where these passages are found. I believe a little nudging from the Universe was the only explanation for my questioning one particular verse so strongly.

After a little searching, I found the Bible that was given to me as a high school graduation present from the church I attended in my youth. It was somewhat fragile, so I carefully opened it to Ecclesiastes 11:6. I was not surprised that the verse had no correlation to the minister's comments, but considering what I had been pondering, I was amazed at what I read: *"In the morning sow thy seed, and in the evening withhold not thine hand: for thou knowest not whether shall prosper, either this or that, or whether they both shall be alike good."* There was my answer. I was not to pick one thing. I was to pursue multiple tasks and let prosper what may. The avenues through which answers come are limitless—and marvelous!

Here is one of my favorite stories. It shows how you can attract wonderfully fun moments to treasure.

I have never been a star-struck person. Although I am one of the biggest movie fans in the world, I would not walk across the street to meet a celebrity, partly because it is not that important and partly because they deserve privacy. However, I had a list of three people whom I admired greatly and would love to meet. One was a former political figure who passed away so my list was down to two. Another was a famous religious leader who had a minor but embarrassing incident that tarnished the halo just enough to fall off my very select list. Now I was down to one: Paul Harvey.

Phoenix is home to many celebrities. After moving here and realizing Paul Harvey had a home here, I decided it was entirely possible for me to meet him. Occasionally I would let ideas roll around in my head as to how this might come about. Now and then I would attempt to find an address so I could write a letter or try to find out if he attended any benefits on a regular basis. Once I even called a television station to see if they had address lists for local celebrities or had a way for forwarding mail to them. I never spent a lot of time on it but I did occasionally mention to people that he is someone I would like to meet. I just held the desire with a "wouldn't it be nice" attitude and a great deal of respect.

In late February 2003, I planned to have lunch with my friend, AnnDee, to celebrate my birthday. First I had to stop at my eleven o'clock doctor's appointment for a quick follow-up check. When I arrived at the doctor's office the clerk said the schedule showed I had a one o'clock appointment, but the doctor was in surgery, so there was no way to see me right then. I looked at my appointment card and it confirmed my appointment was at eleven o'clock, as I had thought.

I was not thrilled at the confusion but it was just a little human error, so I said I would see if my friend could have lunch a little early and I would try to make it back by one o'clock. I was to call the doctor's office ahead of time.

AnnDee was more than happy to meet me early. We met at a place close by for lunch and started having just a wonderful time talking about everything under the sun. When we finished eating, I decided to call the doctor and have them reschedule me. AnnDee and I planned to move on to one of our very favorite places (where we usually meet for lunch) and have a couple of drinks out on the patio.

We had a drink, then decided to walk around and look in some of the shops in this boutique-like shopping and dining area. It was the middle of the afternoon on a Wednesday and we surprisingly had the place almost to ourselves. We stopped at a vacated patio by a coffee shop that was being remodeled and sat down in the sun to enjoy a quiet conversation. One subject led to another and somehow we started talking about all the various celebrities who lived in Phoenix. I told her about the three people I would be honored to meet, that the list was down to one, and that I had tried off and on for years to figure out a way to meet Mr. Harvey.

While listening to her response, a gentleman walking directly toward our table caught my eye. I just stared. He passed within two feet of our table and almost in a daze I said, "AnnDee, I think Paul Harvey just walked by." She gasped with surprise then said, "Oh, Lois. You almost got me with than one—you're good!" She started laughing at what she perceived as a prank. I said softly, "AnnDee. I'm not joking. I think Paul Harvey just walked by. Look at that gentleman walking behind you."

She looked and saw only his back as he was walking away but she got very excited and thought I should go catch up to him. Well, I just did not feel I should do that. He was just out enjoying a beautiful February day in a beautiful spot, the same as we were. A couple of minutes later I looked up and he was walking back toward us. He entered a jewelry store right next to us and AnnDee said, "I'll go look in the window and see if I can tell for sure if it's him." I can still see her standing in front of that shop with the most amazed look and nodding her head affirmatively. She came back to our table, sat down, and could not believe that we had just talked about meeting him and there he was.

A short time later, Mr. Harvey came out of the store and walked directly behind me to pass our table. I could not let this second chance go by. I stood up and the following transpired:

"Excuse me, Sir. Excuse me." He turned and looked. The twinkle in his eye was unmistakable. I asked, "Sir, are you Mr. Paul Harvey?" With a smile and warmth in his voice he said, "I am if you promise not to tell anyone." I assured him his secret was safe with me.

Fortunately there was no one in sight but the three of us. I introduced myself and AnnDee and explained that I was just telling AnnDee how my "people I would like to meet" list had gone from three down to one—him—then I looked up and there you were. He said, "Well. Now you have just made *my* day." I said it would be an honor to shake his hand and he didn't hesitate to extend a friendly handshake.

Mr. Harvey had just flown into Phoenix for the winter and

came directly to one of his favorite places to stroll and enjoy the sunshine—just as AnnDee and I were doing.

There was a multitude of events and atypical decisions made by many people to put me in that place at that moment. Goodness knows how many there were for Mr. Harvey that caused him to be there for his stroll after just flying into town. He even had problems flying out of Chicago because of snow and arrived later than planned. The fact that there were only the three of us in this very popular area for that period of time was also quite amazing.

Thinking beyond the honor, fun, and surprise of meeting Mr. Harvey, I recognized a greater significance. When the Universe presents you with such a special treat, it is confirmation that you are doing something right, that indeed you are being looked after and taken care of. Such events make it easier to know that with a sincere heart all things can work out even better than you imagine.

As stated earlier, I am not star-struck, but I do love autographed books. If I like the subject matter and the author happens to be available for signing, I will go to reasonable lengths to get the autographed book.

Typically my reading materials are educational, inspirational, metaphysical, or biographical. I do not read fiction. There is nothing wrong with fiction. I often wish I could sit and enjoy a good novel and I envy those who can. I have tried but I never get beyond about ten pages. I love fictional drama but I'll take that in cinema format.

A good many years ago when Kirk Douglas wrote his biography, *The Ragman's Son,* I thought it would probably be a very interesting book, but I never got around to buying it. As years went on I heard of other books he wrote and again thought I would probably enjoy reading them. I was especially intrigued to hear that he wrote, *Climbing the Mountain,* a book about his search for meaning and getting back to his spiritual roots. After seeing him on television making references to his book, *My Stroke of Luck,* I instantly had a plan. I would buy *The Ragman's Son, Climbing the*

Mountain, and *My Stroke of Luck* and I would send his most spiritual book, *Climbing the Mountain,* to be autographed by Mr. Douglas. I had a friend who was once an agent for actors and she would be able to help me with this.

I checked with a couple of bookstores but they had none of these books in stock. Of course they could have ordered them but I decided to just keep looking. One afternoon as a friend and I were leaving the Biltmore Plaza shopping area, we passed a bookstore. He suddenly said, "I want to go in here for a minute," and I responded, "Great. I'll look for Kirk Douglas' books."

I looked in the biographies section, I looked in the personal growth section, I looked anywhere I thought they might be, but had no luck. So, as I was milling about waiting for my friend, a store clerk asked if he could help me. I told him I had already looked for my books to no avail. He asked what I wanted. When I told him I was interested in some of Kirk Douglas' books, he said, "Those would be back here in the music department." Who would have guessed? All their celebrity biographies were in a separate room with the music and videos.

He led me back to the correct section and said, "They would be right here. Let's see. We have *The Ragman's Son, Climbing the Mountain,* and *My Stroke of Luck.* It looks like that's all we have." I could hardly believe my ears. Then he said, "Oh, look. *Climbing the Mountain* is an autographed copy."

The sales clerk asked me if any of these would be okay. I said, "I don't even know how to explain to you just how okay they are. Thank you very much for your help. I'll take all three." I purchased the books and left the store with one more miracle in my heart. They never cease to amaze me!

The essence behind many of the stories in this book is that there is more to creating the life you want than just developing specific affirmations and expecting to get exactly what you want. It can happen. However, as the old saying goes, "Be careful what you wish for."

For example, I could have been so fixed on getting a job in

Florida that I was resistant to the changes placed on my path that eventually sent me to Europe where I traveled beyond all my dreams. It would never have occurred to me to ask God to give me a job in Germany. Have your desires, live the best life you can, and leave the details to the Universe. Work with what seem to be obstacles and have faith they will lead you right to where you want to be — or someplace better.

Certainly I could never have created an affirmation or specific desire to have Paul Harvey simply walk by me on a quiet sunny afternoon in a typically busy plaza right while I was talking about my wish to meet him.

As far as Kirk Douglas' autographed book, I didn't even know it was possible to find an autographed copy on the shelf — especially one that had been in print for many years.

Your faith that good begets good, love begets love, and a helping hand begets a helping hand is critical. Core beliefs such as *all things work toward good* are catalysts for the miracle-making process — the power behind your affirmations and visualizations. Doing good and expecting good must come as naturally as expecting the sun to rise each day and that April will bring rain. Do not keep score! Avoid thinking, "I did good things for Janey so she owes me a favor." The Universe keeps detailed accounts and your good can come from the most surprising sources at the most perfect time — much better than a return favor from Janey. Good given by your right hand can be returned to your left hand. One can never know for sure when one small act of kindness is your opportunity to trigger a chain of events that leads to something spectacular.

Chapter Thirteen
The Big Picture

I do not think turning one's life around to create a positive, loving environment where miracles can flourish is all that difficult. It is like any other skill or trade—you just need to know how. It does take discipline, but mostly it takes desire—you have to *decide* on a new way. In every second of every day you are making decisions. You decide to get out of bed, speak, sit or stand, eat, shower, get the mail, walk around the block, or use the phone. So before you even get out of bed, *decide* it is going to be a great day. Before you speak, *decide* to be pleasant and kind. Before you sit or stand, decide that your presence will have a positive impact. While showering, imagine the water washing away any negativity or limiting thoughts. On your way to the mailbox expect good things and before talking on the phone consciously bless the person on the other end and decide the conversation will be kind and mutually beneficial.

You have to really want to make changes. You have to recognize there's a better way of thinking and living. You have to recognize that your own words and behavior contribute significantly to every single outcome in your life. You have to want joy and happiness more than you want the perpetual contests of life, such as having the last word, showing someone you are smarter or that you own more stuff, getting back at the people you care most about just because they hurt your feelings, blaming others for your actions, or justifying selfishness. When you learn to bring the right thoughts into your mind, the right feelings will come into your heart and you will be amazed at how quickly such conflicting episodes will fade away. Nature abhors a vacuum, so when negative or critical thoughts are interrupted, there is room for good thoughts to come rushing in ever so easily. It is nothing more or less than a conscious choice of behavior.

Imagine yourself standing at a fixed point and looking straight ahead. You can see many things and you are able to form a good description of where you are. Picture yourself turning in the opposite direction and looking straight ahead. You now see totally different images and your description of "where you are" would probably be dramatically different. That is what happens when you choose to see and react to life from the affirmative. You will not need to change every little thing around you, although every little thing around you will change. Do not wait for your world to change—change yourself and your world will experience the most amazing changes right before your eyes.

Although it may seem like changing a myriad of behaviors, think of it as flipping over a coin. There is a totally different image with many different details, but all you did was flip the coin over. Flip your thoughts and attitudes over to positive, expecting great things.

For the sake of clarity we are going to look at some of those details you will encounter when you flip that positive switch. I believe with all my heart that many people do not even realize they are being negative and putting out fruitless, or worse yet, destructive energy. I know this because I used to do so by worrying. Worrying is thinking about the worst possible outcome. Remember, our thoughts create! No matter how nice, generous, and forgiving you may be, worrying puts forth energy to create difficult circumstances. This is an example of how bad things can happen to very nice people. Many of us need to be shown how to create positive energy — sometimes these ways are too simple to recognize on our own. Equally important is the prevention of creating negative or neutralizing energy. As humans we often tend to overlook the obvious.

Starting Your Day: Before you get out of bed in the morning, give thanks for the day, make a positive statement about what a wonderful day it will be, and then smile. Somewhere along the way most of us bought into the consciousness that we must have something immediately at hand to smile about, or we do not do it. Just smile, and keep smiling the entire time you are preparing to meet your day. If you do this, people around you will respond in kind and your day will have started very well. If you just keep smiling, many of you will find yourself singing in the shower or humming to the radio on the way to work. Smiling takes very little effort, it feels good all throughout your body, and it can change your entire day. Smile right now. Feel better?

Before I rise, usually before my eyes are even open, I say affirmations: *Thank You for today and all that it may bring. Help me be kind all day. Today will be harmonious and productive.* They vary according to what my plans are. If I have a meeting, I might say the following: *I meet only kind, cooperative people today.* Say it, believe it, expect it.

Take Responsibility: Until you take responsibility for your experiences you will no doubt continue to find yourself in difficult or unpleasant conditions for which you also continue to blame others.

I once had a male colleague with whom I had a very strange working relationship, as he did with many other employees. We interacted frequently in our daily accomplishments and he invariably seemed cold and uncooperative. On the surface, and by almost anyone's account, he appeared to be the cause of the uncomfortable working condition. However, understanding my own accountability for my circumstances, I decided to take full responsibility for the situation and give it my spiritual focus.

Determined to be the best colleague that I could be, I began visualizing him sitting in his office with a smile on his face and surrounded by a mist or cloud of pink (pink being the color of pure love). If a negative thought came to mind, I replaced it with this affirmation: *We always work pleasantly and productively together.*

Very quickly I found myself thinking about the traits that I did admire and respect about this gentleman. The next time he approached my desk I greeted him with a smile. It went well and as he walked away I said, "You know, I've been meaning to tell you I really respect the way you handled that last personnel issue." He knew what I referred to and after a moment of surprise he smiled and said, "Thank you."

The next time I went to his office I mentally flooded the room with pink light and said, "I could use some advice." I sat down and asked his opinion on a particular purchase I was working on for the company. Ever after, he was the most cordial and supportive co-worker I had. I had taken responsibility for this work relationship, added some positive thoughts, spiritual energy, and old fashioned kindness. I desired a change, visualized a change, used words of praise and respect, and change came. I did not change the situation. I changed me and watched the rest change around me.

Brief Encounters: All day long we have personal contact with other people. If you are not engaged in a profession where you have constant contact with colleagues, your encounters may be with the grocery clerk, the receptionist at your physician's office, your child's teacher, or someone in the parking lot of a business where you are going for a job interview. This last example should not be treated too lightly—it could be the person with whom you are about to meet. It has happened to me.

Even those of you who are not typically rude to people in such brief encounters might be able to do better. The next time you walk up to a ticket booth at the movies, do not appear too rushed to be nice. At the checkout line in the grocery, deliberately smile and give a nice "hello" instead of just digging through your coupons with a distracted squint on your face. "Thanks, have a nice day," is always a good departure. What if an airline ticket clerk had just been spoken to in a demeaning way and she was about to quit her job? Your friendly exchange could be what makes her feel valued and might help her put the other comments into perspective. Have you ever encountered someone who was all smiles and cheery and when he (or she) left you turned to another person and said, "That sure was a friendly person, wasn't he (or she)?" And you said it with a smile on your face and you felt good. I assure you the person did not just happen to be a happy individual because life had been so wonderful on this particular day. It was a conscious choice of behavior and you can do the same. Just behave it and you will feel it. So will everyone around you—everyone will then behave differently, which will affect others and so on. Go ahead—make a ripple!

Traffic: Got your attention, didn't I? This one is tough for almost everyone. I was in traffic when I first began using a technique that I later learned was called mirroring. It is about recalling yourself in a comparable situation as the other person. All you need is a desire to do this and the examples where you may have behaved quite similarly will come flying into your consciousness. It gets a little tough to criticize someone when you remember behaving the same way yourself. It is truly putting yourself in another's shoes.

For me, traffic was an ever-present opportunity to practice mirroring. In difficult traffic I could use language that otherwise never tainted my lips. I am not proud of this, but I am proud that it stopped completely with one particular encounter.

While driving along a two-way traffic road that was a little hilly and curvy, I came up behind a car going about thirty-five miles per hour. It was early in the evening and there were no other cars in sight. I was quite familiar with this road and its traffic patterns and I was extremely tempted to pass, but it was getting dark, there was a double yellow line, and my intellect would not let me do anything that stupid. I took a moment to reflect on the fact that I only seem to be behind a slow driver when I am in a great rush. Realizing I was stuck for about the next five miles, I clinched the steering wheel and made some growling throaty noise. At that point I realized I needed to replace my thoughts.

No sooner did my mind blink out the question, "What can I think to make this all right?" when a very clear picture came into mind. About ten years earlier, I had taken ill and had to drive myself to the hospital. I was slumped over the steering wheel in severe pain and crying as I drove down the dark country road, only moving at about fifteen miles an hour. Everyone coming up behind me was sounding their horn. As they passed they were even less polite. I hated causing the situation and felt a need to explain the situations to everyone who passed.

As that picture came to mind, all anxiety left me. My only thought was the realization that I had no idea what was going on in the car in front of me. As soon as my thoughts changed to a more positive and understanding position, the car in front of me pulled onto the shoulder of the road and waved me by. As I drove by I noticed it was an elderly couple. Perhaps they almost never drove and were on their way to a hospital, just old people doing the best they could. I prayed that they would safely get to wherever they were going. I waved a friendly "thank you" as I passed them.

The next time someone cuts in front of you in traffic, instead of getting upset, I feel pretty sure you can recall a time when you cut over not realizing how close another vehicle was. If someone slams on their brakes in front of you because he or she was apparently not paying attention to cars ahead, I think you could probably remember a time or two you took your eyes off the road and had to stop suddenly. If you cannot quite put yourself on the other side of a traffic situation, try a protective statement such as, "I arrive timely and safely."

Pay attention, do your best, and God will do the rest. Patience with other drivers will also make us safer drivers. Let that be our biggest concern.

If you run into a delay or detour, just give thanks. Trust Divine timing and accept that this situation may be keeping you from a serious accident farther up the street where the Universe knows someone is about to run a red light. I say the prayer of protection every time I get in my car. If I expect protection I must accept that any event along the way could be engaging that protection.

One day I had a flat tire on Interstate 10 in one of the highest traffic areas of Phoenix. I said the prayer of protection as I pulled off to the side and almost immediately a family stopped to help. I took a deep breath and affirmed that this delay had a positive purpose. A kind gentleman and his son changed my tire and I was gratefully on my way in hardly any time at all. About fifteen miles up the road I passed a very serious, multi-car accident that had just happened. Would I have been in that serious situation had I not had my flat tire? Or what about the people who stopped to help me? Since one of my standard affirmations is "I'm always in the right place at the right time," perhaps the Universe used me as a willing participant in a plan to prevent such a thoughtful family from a serious situation.

General Affirmations: One can make a very fun game out of looking for the positive. There are many situations when the best one can say is, "Good will come from this." Saying this statement with complete conviction, over and over, can bring you up and out of many adversities with astounding results. Sometimes we cannot imagine what those good results might be. In such cases, do not limit God by being too specific. There have been times when I laughed, threw up my hands, and said, "I can't wait to see the good that comes from this one!"

Signs: There are always signs to let us know we are being watched over. Examples of this are scattered throughout this book. However, signs will not typically knock you over the head and say, "Here's a sign!" I do not believe in spending time looking for signs, but what works for me is expecting them. Know they will be there and just pay attention to your life.

It is my nature to be observant and give extraordinary thought to everything going on around me. Others are less philosophical and think in more pragmatic details. I can only offer one simple technique for using the guidance of signs offered to us: When you see something unusual or profound, take a moment to consider what you were thinking about just before that, or about any major situation going on in your life. Then see if you can draw any correlation or pull any helpful wisdom from the event. This is a totally personal and subjective matter. Beyond this I can only offer examples.

One day when I was in my early twenties, I was looking in a mirror and brushing my hair when something outside caught my eye. Looking out the window, which was right beside the mirror, I saw an elderly lady pushing a wheelchair. In the wheelchair was a very young man who wore braces from head to toe. The elderly lady struggled to get the wheelchair down over the curb, across the street and up the curb on the other side. I watched until they were out of sight.

While brushing my hair I had been feeling very sad and tired. After watching every detail of the struggle going on outside the window, I easily saw many positives in my life and I found new strength. I had been reminded of what a gift it was to be young, whole, and healthy, and of the potential—potential to change circumstances—which I had that others may not have. I inquired around and no one knew of anyone in a wheelchair in the neighborhood. Wherever they came from they were just what I needed.

I was recently involved in a business situation that had the potential of becoming very difficult. I said a quick prayer for a sign that all would go well. I walked from my bedroom into the living area and there in the middle of the floor was a white feather. I have no feather pillows, all the doors and windows were closed because of the Arizona heat, and I had just recently walked across that area. As white feathers have frequently been signs for me, I said my thanks and proceeded with confidence.

Keep in mind that when you start making deep personal changes, things around you will begin to change. Some of this will be obviously wonderful. Some relationships will heal, better working conditions may "just happen," and your energy levels will probably skyrocket. Conversely, some of the changes will appear difficult and you will wonder why on earth you are having such difficulty after making so many positive changes. Affirm your strength to get through the situation and affirm your faith that all things work toward good. It may be necessary to experience loss to make way for something new and better.

It is equally important to be mindful that you never know what act of kindness, tolerance or generosity will tip the karmic merit/demerit scale and trigger a chain of events that will create just the miraculous outcome you need. Go forth and play nice.

Yes, but: What if your employer walked up to you and said, "We would like to promote you to the Junior Executive position we have open in Colorado." After you have said, "Thank you, that's an exciting offer," would your next thoughts be, "What a great opportunity to consider," or would it be, "Yes, but I'd have to sell the house, packing will be a nightmare, and I don't know anyone there"? As you learn to react positively to great opportunities, you will attract more of them to you. Be open to your highest good and it will move toward you. As I always say, "Put your boat in the water—God will steer it."

You will be amazed at the differences in the way you think, feel, and respond to situations if you just learn to rephrase. Instead of "I hope," try "I trust." Instead of "I can't," or "I don't know how," try "I'm not sure at this moment how I will do that," or "Give me a little time to check out the best approach to that."

We have all heard the expression "walk the talk." Although it is intended to convey a different and very important point, I assure you we all *do* walk the talk. Our "talk" creates the very path we trod.

Making Room for Your Miracles: As they say, ships come in over still waters. It takes a calm and controlled mind to create your miraculous life. Confused, stressed, indecisive thoughts give the Universe confused, stressed, indecisive signals. I have learned over the years that one of the most important things you can do for your mental, physical, and emotional well-being is to have some quiet time. Everyone has a different reason for being so busy and much of it may be just habit. In general, people have forgotten how to be alone without being lonely. Perhaps some fail to understand the difference.

> In the Silence I can hear,
> God erasing all my fear.
> When sounds depart, He's in my heart
> His love and grace I then draw near.
> The Silence whispers a secret knowing.
> A better way of living it's showing.
> It says let go of the negative flow,
> And feel your spirit growing.
> —Lois A. Enochs

You will find it extremely beneficial to create time for stillness. I do not necessarily mean a strict regimen of meditation—which is great if you can do it—but just some quiet time. My most regular quiet time is in my car. Unless there is a good reason, the radio is never turned on. There are no CDs and I put effort into imagining pleasantries and saying affirmations.

Another of my favorites is excellent for housewives and mothers: If you spend most of your day communicating at the toddler level and your thoughts are consumed with the needs of others all day, get Dad to take charge of the kids for an hour or so and lock yourself away for a bubble bath. Spend your time thinking about how soothing the warm water feels on your skin. Breathe in the fragrant bath oils and actually think about the aroma. Wash your skin with bath salts and remain aware that this is *your* time. Do not think about tomorrow's TO DO list or what you will have for dinner on Friday. By the time you have finished your quiet time and returned to your family you will feel and behave like a new person.

Exercise is a great way to get the mind off the everyday mental clutter—if you exercise alone. I see many people go with friends to the gym and the entire time is spent yapping about their problems—not much of a break there. If you enjoy movies, go alone. True, the mind is still busy with the movie, but it is totally refocused from the mental rhetoric of your daily life, so it can be quite beneficial. If you have a porch swing, spend some time on it doing absolutely nothing. Let your mind wander but steer it away from anything unpleasant or stressful. Recall happy events!

These are good times to work with general affirmations regarding health and happiness. The quiet time will allow you to start intuiting good choices and create the calm seas over which will come the miracles of your making.

Time with no input from others and no need to respond to others is what is important here. It is you with your own thoughts. It is you with nature. It is you with whatever creative power you believe in. You will get to know what you believe, what you really think (not what others want you to think), and what you really want. Now *that* is a really good starting point.

Many times we overlook opportunities for "the quiet." The next time you have a little time at home alone, be sure the television and radio are off. When the family is watching a show you do not especially enjoy, fix a drink and go sit on the patio. If possible, take evening walks. On occasion, instead of calling a friend for lunch and shopping, go alone. You just might be amazed at the things you find yourself thinking about and equally amazed at what you don't think about.

Think carefully, speak carefully, and behave appropriately. Bless those around you who cause you difficulties. Always picture them surrounded in pink light and watch changes unfold. Hold your desires close to your heart and have faith that your highest good will come. Allow difficult people and situations to move from your life as you evolve. Keep your surroundings in order. Quiet your mind so you can notice the changes around you, so you can get to know your own heart, and recognize your miracles — for they can appear as but a whisper.

My desire for those who read my material or hear me speak

is a life richer than money alone can provide,

experiences beyond what you've imagined,

and love that is beyond self,

beyond passion,

and beyond human expression.

May your cup runneth over.

The End

is only the beginning

To the Reader

Let Lois know your favorite part of the book
and how it affected you.

Subscribe to her newsletter
The Light Post
($16 check or money order for one-year subscription)

Order an **autographed** copy of this book
($18.50 check or money order includes shipping)

Write to:

Lois Enochs
PO Box 8303
Phoenix, AZ 85066

Email:

MiraclesAndYou@msn.com
or
TheLightPost@msn.com